101 RUMS

TO TRY BEFORE YOU DIE

101 RUMS

TO TRY BEFORE YOU DIE

IAN BUXTON

BIRLINN

First published in Great Britain in 2018
by Birlinn Ltd
West Newington House
10 Newington Road
Edinburgh
EH9 1QS

www.birlinn.co.uk

ISBN: 978 1 78027 544 4
Copyright © Ian Buxton, 2018

British Library Cataloguing-in-Publication Data
A catalogue record for this book is available on request from
the British Library

Designed by Teresa Monachino
Printed and bound by Livonia Print, Latvia

CONTENTS

INTRODUCTION

Perhaps it's the funk, or the hogo, or the thunder of the dunder[1], but whatever's going on, rum is definitely having a moment. Rum, after centuries in the doldrums, is once again a *thing*.

But what sort of thing, because there's no denying that rum can be confusing. There are a confusing number of styles. Do you, for example, prefer your rum in the British, French or Spanish style? Do you refer to it by colour? White – or silver, as some would have it – gold or dark might be your guide. And where do you stand on the vexed question of added sugar: is it a sweet benediction or the work of the Devil?

Does rum have to come from the Caribbean? In fact, it's made virtually everywhere that sugar cane is grown and quite a few places where it isn't, unless I've missed Orkney's lush and verdant sugar fields. Rum is made – pause for impressive list – all across the Caribbean; in Central and Latin America; Canada and the USA; much of Africa; Australia; India and in the islands of the Indian Ocean; Japan; the Philippines; Nepal; Thailand; parts of Europe; England; and, yes, even in bonnie Scotland. And, as things stand, I've probably missed a good few (Albanian rum, anyone? It could well be out there). Once upon a time rum was a major industry in New England. Its remarkable geographic spread is part of rum's appeal and yet, as we shall see, one of its challenges.

Then there's the question of the stills. Some swear by the product of the pot still; others are aficionados of the traditional column; while yet a third school maintains the superiority of the modern multi-column still. Or, as many do, you can blend the spirit from different types of stills – and why not, because the results can be delicious. And though most rum is made from molasses, if this book were published in France, the automatic assumption would be that it was made, *naturellement*, with fresh sugar cane juice. Strangely though, sugar beet alcohol, despite some small experiments, is not generally accepted as rum.

Cane sugar is also used to produce cachaça (sometimes termed Brazilian Rum), clairin (native to Haiti), aguardiente (Andean South America), arrack (Asia; rice and other additives may be added to the distillation) and basi (from the Philippines). Not to be purist, but as

---

these are rarely if ever seen in the UK, apart from clairin they fall outside the scope of this book. And, because it's anathema to hardcore rum snobs, dare we mention spiced rum?

Actually, though, why not? Spiced rum can claim a great heritage and some of today's most exciting and innovative rum-based drinks are a play on spiced rum. What's more, the popular brands of spiced rums bring new drinkers into the category and, potentially, introduce them to the amazing world of this most versatile of spirits. If you accept rum as a key ingredient in classic cocktails, as even the most hardline and pedantic stickler seems to do, then I can't see the problem that some commentators have with spiced rum. But while you'll find a few of the best listed here, the Captain is missing in action.

By contrast, one of the most interesting products in this book, supplies of which should be reaching the UK around about the time this goes to print, is a twenty-first-century take on a very traditional spiced rhum agricole or clairin trempé from Haiti (see entry 21 – Boukman).

However, though this probably isn't a book for purists, even they will be pleased that I've drawn the line at flavoured rums. There is so much flavour in good rum to start with that added flavourings such as torched cherry, wolfberry (no, I've no idea either) and coffee rum (why, just why?) seem uncalled for. If flavoured alcohol is what you want, then look in the vodka aisle, as there will certainly be something there for your inner adolescent, but please, step away from the rum.

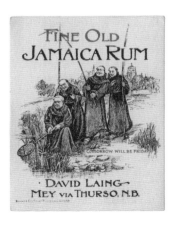

That said, I couldn't resist including one particular pineapple-infused rum that comes with stellar credentials. It's based on a recipe mentioned by Charles Dickens who, as far as I'm aware, never extolled the virtues of torched cherry or coffee rum. If 'hot pine-apple rum-and-water' was good enough for Boz then it's certainly good enough for me.

In my listings I've attempted a spread of style, origin, colour and flavour. I've tried to point out that great rum doesn't need to be mixed with cola (in fact, I'd rather you didn't do that) or even used in a cocktail – tasty and enjoyable as some of these really are – but can be enjoyed exactly as you would a fine cognac or Scotch whisky.

Actually, that's part of the reason for rum's rapidly growing popularity. An ever-increasing number of whisky drinkers, especially those who in the past might have favoured single malt Scotch, have grown disenchanted with whisky's increasingly desperate attempts to play with the trendy kids. As whisky has become more fashionable, so demand has risen and, inexorably, so have prices; a trend that has been further compounded by shortages of mature stock and ever more lavish and costly (not to say, vulgar) packaging. A move by many producers to drop age declarations in favour of No Age Statement (or NAS) bottlings has not been universally well received, and more than a few traditionally minded whisky consumers have begun to look around for the combination of flavour, rich heritage and value that once characterised Scotch.

Realising, belatedly, that's there more to rum than rum and Coke, many have ended up exploring and savouring a world of outstanding quality rums which, currently, offer remarkable value for money. Having said that, there are some alarming signs that certain distillers (or their marketing departments) have looked with greedy eyes at whisky pricing. But despite that worrying development, it's still very hard indeed to find a rum at anything over £1,000 a bottle and, rare antiquities and limited-edition commemoratives aside, there is nothing currently available on the UK market at more than £3,500. Even Havana Club's remarkable Máximo Extra (number 49) could be yours for under £1,250. It is the most expensive rum in the book, but I have made an extra-special effort on your behalf and tasted it. You can thank me later.

Agreed, £1,000 is a great deal of money for anything, let alone a bottle of grog, but consider this: a 60-year-old single malt such as Glenfarclas will cost around £15,000; a 1926 Dalmore will set you back over £50,000 and a collection of The Macallan Six Pillars (basically six bottles, but admittedly in Lalique decanters) sold recently for just shy of $1 million.

In comparison, you can find the 1929 bottling of Bally's rhum agricole from Martinique for under £2,000 or unbroached flagons of Royal Navy rum from the 1960s for the bottle equivalent of £350.

It won't last. The smart 'investment' money has already spotted the opportunity in rum: dusty old bottles are starting to appear on the main online auction sites and prices are moving up. If you want to get into this game, names to look out for are J. Wray & Nephew, the Italian bottler Samaroli, Caroni, Port Mourant, Uitvlugt, Long Pond and early bottles from Barbancourt.

But here's the good news: there are many, many fantastic rums to enjoy at well under £100 a bottle. In fact, you'll find particularly good value in the £30–50 price range, so enjoy.

A World to Explore

As I've mentioned, rum is made across the globe and this is a great part of its appeal. It can also be a challenge, leading to confusion in labelling and some misconceptions as to what actually constitutes rum. It's a complex subject, and what follows represents a considerable simplification. If you want a basic introduction, then read on. If you can't be bothered, then just jump right into the rums. Otherwise take a deep breath and, if you actually know about this stuff, please excuse my sweeping approach.

Due in part to rum's colourful history (and there are whole books on this as well), we can identify three basic styles: English, Spanish and French. These can be related to the respective nation's colonial past and are thus inextricably linked to a darker record of imperial conquest, slavery and oppression, as European powers looked to dominate the Caribbean sugar trade through the infamous 'triangular trade'. However fascinating, these are not topics that I have space to cover here, though there are passing references where they are relevant to individual brand stories.

Something else that crops up all the time is piracy. The association of pirates and rum remains a potent one, as illustrated by the number of brands that maintain a somewhat romanticised connection with these brigands. In actual fact, pirates were (and remain) deeply unpleasant and violent characters, best avoided in real life. Back in the past they undoubtedly drank anything they could beg, borrow or steal, and whether they cruised the waters of the Caribbean or New England, then rum would have been just part of their provisions. We can thank Robert Louis Stevenson's novel *Treasure Island* and his Long John Silver character for much of the misrepresentation of the pirate in popular culture whilst noting, in passing, that however misplaced the imagery it is certainly enduring and retains a widespread appeal.

> Fifteen men on the dead man's chest—
> Yo-ho-ho, and a bottle of rum!
> Drink and the devil had done for the rest—
> Yo-ho-ho, and a bottle of rum!

Stevenson only ever mentions the chorus to the pirate's song and seems to have taken the 'dead man's chest' reference from Dead Chest Island, the name of a tiny, uninhabited rock outcrop, part of the British Virgin Islands. The story of Blackbeard marooning a mutinous crew there with a bottle of rum and a cutlass each post-dates Stevenson's novel, but speaks to the potency of the pirate mythology.

In what Disney's film trailer would refer to as 'the world's greatest adventure story', the actor Robert Newton, himself no stranger to a hard-drinking lifestyle, portrayed Silver with the exaggerated West Country accent that spawned the archetypal pirate's voice and subsequently inspired the creation of International Talk Like A Pirate Day. It's every 19 September, should you feel the need to borrow a parrot for the day and hail chums and shipmates with cries of 'Ahoy, me hearties!'

While the link between pirates and rum may be spurious, it is undeniably potent and seems unlikely to fade. Perhaps a more positive association would be between rum and revolution, notably the American War of Independence, the Haitian Revolution and Australia's less well-known Rum Rebellion of 1808. However, this is not a history book, so on to a brief and very broad-brush summary of the principal geographical styles.

Modern Cuban

Basically, this is a shorthand way to describe Bacardi and similar white rums. As the best-known brand on the UK market, Bacardi is many consumers' introduction to the spirit but, ironically, is somewhat atypical. Originating in Cuba during the nineteenth century, it is today made principally in Puerto Rico in a modern multi-column continuous distillation process, resulting in a very clean, light-bodied, less assertive rum, which is aged in oak barrels but then filtered to remove the colour. In its younger versions (Carta Blanca and Carta Oro), it is well suited to mixing and is promoted on the basis of its historic association with Cuba and as a party and lifestyle brand.

Bacardi in particular has been an outstanding marketing achievement; such is the potency of the brand that it is not entirely clear if every Bacardi drinker would necessarily know that it was rum they were drinking.

English – Rum

An earlier, and thus today, more traditional style of rum for the English market originated from the British colonies in the Caribbean and tended to a heavier, molasses-dominated taste, which varies by island origin. Rums from Jamaica and Guyana, often distilled in traditional pots similar to those used for malt whisky, were heavier, richer and more full-flavoured when compared to the style which predominated in Barbados. Navy Rum was a blend from different distilleries to a specification drawn up by the Admiralty.

Spanish – Ron

Spain once had extensive colonies in the West Indies and in Central and South America, where expatriate Spanish distillers introduced their distilling techniques and the use of the solera system found in sherry production from home, notably in the Jerez region. Hence, Spanish-influenced rums tend to a sweeter, fruitier taste, somewhat reminiscent of brandy. Many Spanish-style rums contain a percentage

of added sugar, a practice entirely legal in some jurisdictions yet completely banned elsewhere (e.g. Barbados). The addition of sugar is increasingly controversial and the operation of a typical rum distillery's solera has, over time, diverged somewhat from the practice in Jerez.

French – Rhum

The classic French tradition is rather different. For the most part, distillation is of fermented sugarcane juice subsequently distilled in smaller, single-column stills. This is known as rhum agricole and is widely found in rums sold in France, which remains a very important market for rum, especially this distinctive style. These rhum agricoles originate largely from the French West Indies, particularly Martinique, and the Indian Ocean French colonies. It also remains the dominant style for artisanal production in the former French colony of Haiti. The taste is quite different to other rums, being in general grassier, dryer and somewhat vegetal. If accustomed to the other styles, the first taste of rhum agricole may come as something of a shock.

Because rum is produced so widely and in line with quite distinct traditions, there is no one common method of classification. Attempts to classify by colour are overly simplistic, and the ageing of rum is an area fraught with problems, not least because of the solera system. For that reason alone, it is important to study the label closely: many solera-aged rums carry a prominent number on the label, which the unwary, or those familiar with the more strictly regulated world of whisky, might easily assume to be an age statement in years. It is not always so! Quite apart from that, as rum producers are quick to point out, the typical maturation conditions of most rums result in a significantly faster ageing than found in most whiskies. As a consequence, it is relatively unusual to find rum that has been aged for an extended period – a 20 or 25-year-old rum is something of an exception to the general rule and a 50 or 60-year-old rum is a real rarity.

Distillers have long since sought to accelerate the ageing process, with a sharp eye to the considerable profits that could be obtained from getting the flavour without all the tedious and costly delays involved in casks and warehouses. So far, no one has achieved anything close to satisfactory, but there is a rum here (Lost Spirits – 54) that may be about to change the whole spirits industry.

Classifying Rum

It would seem that proposing a definitive system of rum classification is a thankless and demanding task, but that does not stop people trying. Perhaps the nearest anyone has come to it is the system proposed by Luca Gargano of Velier (an influential Italian independent bottler) and forcefully endorsed by Foursquare Rum's Master Distiller, Richard Seale. The Gargano Rum Classification System has yet to be widely used, but it is gaining some credence amongst dedicated enthusiasts. The problem it faces is that it is unlikely to be adopted by the major international competitions or industry giants such as Diageo or Bacardi, who will likely be unimpressed with their less-than-appealing description as 'modern/industrial', however accurate it may well be. Doubtless they will also see the classification as promoting the self-interests of Gargano and Seale, and there is some justice in that charge.

For all that, the Gargano classification is surely superior to the confusion of classification by colour and has the great merit of simplicity. Here are his proposed categories:

Pure Single Rum – Molasses 100% Batch Pot Still Distillation
Pure Single Agricole Rhum – Cane Juice 100% Batch Pot Still Distillation
Single Blended Rum – Blend of 100% Traditional Column and Pot Still rums
Traditional Rum – Traditional 100% Column Still Distillation
Modern Rum – Modern / Industrial Multi-Column Distillation
Pure 100% Pot Still rum
Single 100% Single Distillery rum

This may gather momentum in future years as a growing band of enthusiasts demand more and more information about the products they are drinking. This has happened with other spirits and will surely come to influence rum packaging and brand communication. Right now, what is probably most important is that people understand what they are drinking; hopefully this *101 Rums to Try Before You Die* will make some small contribution to that process.

The format here follows that of my previous efforts in the *101 Whiskies* series and the more recent *101 Gins to Try Before You Die*. On the left-hand page is a large picture[2] of the bottle under discussion, with some

---

2   But be aware that those pesky marketing folks are forever changing both label and bottle designs; damn their eyes.

brief pointers to further information. Opposite is my commentary on what struck me as important, interesting or different about the rum in question. I've aimed to be approachable and not overly serious, and what you get is a personal view. As I never tire of repeating, it's only a drink we're discussing, not politics, religion or nuclear chemistry. If it's not fun, then I maintain that we've rather lost sight of the point.

And, as ever, there are no scores or particularly lengthy tasting notes. I don't know what you like, and what I like is only one person's opinion. Your opinion is rather more important to you, as it should be, so try lots of things and go from there. It's basically what I do…

Five o'clock Rum

1

ADMIRAL RODNEY
EXTRA OLD

Brand owner: St Lucia Distillers
Website: www.saintluciarums.com
Origin: St Lucia

ONE OF THE LOVELY THINGS ABOUT RUM IS THAT DIFFERENT RUMS frequently come with interesting history lessons, and I find that it adds to my enjoyment to discover the backstory behind a particular brand name.

This tasty drop from St Lucia Distillers, on the lovely island of the same name, carries the moniker of Admiral Rodney. Who he, you plonker? Well, as you can't be bothered to look it up, he was a very distinguished eighteenth-century British admiral, who was so successful in various naval battles against the French that he was made a peer and granted a life pension of £2,000 annually. By one measure, that's worth more than £21 million today, so you can see that he was very highly thought of by his contemporaries.

The award was principally for his achievements at the Battle of the Saintes (April 1782) which, among other things, prevented a French invasion of the important colony of Jamaica and also saved the Windward Islands group, including St Lucia. Strange though it now seems, Britain's Caribbean interests were then thought more valuable than the 13 American colonies, so considerable importance was attached to their defence during the American War of Independence (the colonists were aided by the French).

So, consider this: had Admiral Sir George Brydges Rodney not given the Comte de Grasse and his 35 ships of the line a jolly good thrashing, St Lucia might have become French and we'd be drinking rhum agricole. But Rodney was keen on his prize money (rather too keen, according to many contemporaries), and fittingly, this Admiral Rodney rum has been filling its boots with honours.

Rightly so, because this is a nicely matured and very well-made rum from the charming St Lucia distillery. It's described as 'Extra Old', which seems rather vague, but upon further enquiry I have established that the rums used have an average age of 12 years, and the distillery hopes that future releases will see that increase to 15 years. It's very much the company's flagship product and a fine example of an aged rum from molasses and a continuous still.

It's unsweetened, but naturally delivers quite a honeyed, rich and mouth-coating palate. At around £50 it's definitely one for sipping while reflecting on the glorious history of our past naval victories (unless you're reading this in France, obviously).

2

ALDI'S OLD HOPKING WHITE

Brand owner: Aldi Stores Ltd
Website: www.aldi.co.uk
Origin: Blend

NOW, LET'S BE HONEST. YOU'RE WATCHING THE TELLY AND PROBABLY snacking on crisps (though you know you shouldn't). Some friends – not terribly discriminating drinkers, if truth be told – have popped by for a chat. Or perhaps it's sunny and you're chilling in the garden.

There are some days when all you want from your rum is a pleasant hit of alcohol; a bit of complexity and depth and a sensible price. After all, it's not every day that you want or need to think deeply about what you're drinking; to sip and savour the subtleties of some arcane spirit or to impress your drinking buddies with your superior connoisseurship. Some days you just want a drink.

This may just hit the spot. It may come in at a modest 37.5% ABV but, tasted neat, it drinks fuller than that, and in practical terms all it means is that your chosen mixer goes further because you won't be using as much. And there's more good news: at the time of writing, the price of a full bottle is under a tenner. So, what's not to like?

Well, the curious Old Hopking brand name, I suppose. I must admit to some confusion when I first encountered this, assuming it was a craft beer. So confused was I that I asked their helpful PR person where the name came from. Normally, if they don't know, you get some PR obfuscation and a more-or-less convincing attempt to make something up. Bearing this in mind, I was delighted to learn that (and I quote directly from the email) 'unfortunately the current buyers inherited the product, so don't know where the name "Old Hopking" comes from! One of life's mysteries"☺)'.

And so it must remain, but I particularly appreciated the smiley face.

Ignore the basic bottle and label, ignore the drinks snobs who may look down on this and grab a bargain. If challenged, point out that this won a perfectly decent silver medal in the 2016 International Wine & Spirits Competition (IWSC) and it is a genuine Caribbean rum, originating in Trinidad and Tobago (here endeth the Bluffer's Guide). Or get your picky friends to taste it blind in a line-up of two or three other better-known white rums – that should shut them up.

Or tell them it cost less than a tenner (did I mention the price already?). Then put on your best smiley face.

3

ANGOSTURA 1919

Brand owner: Angostura Holdings
Website: www.angosturarum.com
Origin: Trinidad

LONG REVERED FOR FINE RUM AND FOR ITS EPONYMOUS BITTERS
– an essential in any cocktail cabinet – this Trinadadian producer
has emerged from some tortuous commercial wrangling to again
concentrate on the products that made it famous. If you're wondering
where the name came from, it was actually Venezuala, where in 1824
in the town of Angostura (now Ciudad Bolívar), Dr J. G. B. Siegert
invented his aromatic bitters while working as Surgeon General to
the armies of Simón Bolívar.

Later, to escape Venezuala's penal taxes, the family moved to Trinidad
and distilled rum on a small scale. Things really took off in the 1940s
but, confusingly, this 1919 expression relates to events in 1932, when
the Government Rum Bond burnt down. Some heavily charred casks
survived the fire and the master blender of Fernandes Distillers, J. B.
Fernandes, bought them. They dated from 1919 and, one presumes,
the combination of their great age and their exposure to the heat,
flame and smoke of the conflagration had produced something quite
unusual. I'd love to tell you that ancient casks of rum are still left
to the tender mercies of some pyromaniac in the hope of Vulcan's
favourable intercession, but nothing so romantic actually occurs
(though it's an idea . . .).

So, though Angostura 1919 may celebrate a very particular date
in the development of the rum industry in Trinidad and Tobago,
today the product is sadly only a tribute to that remarkable original.
However, though its creation is no longer a matter of serendipity, it
is still a notable achievement, employing Angostura's large five-
column distillation plant, with lengthy ageing in specially charred
barrels. As to the exact age, eight years is often quoted, though I
have been unable to verify this and other sources suggest this is a
blend of five to ten-year-old rums. It scarcely matters, for this is well
matured without being over-aged or woody, with the molasses fading
discreetly into the background.

The result is a beautifully well-mannered and complex spirit, creamy
sweet on initial impact but revealing crème brûlée notes alongside
cocoa, caramel, buttered toast and ripe bananas. This is not quite top
of the line for Angostura (they also offer a couple of higher-priced
expressions), but I would suggest that you can buy this confident that
no bitter surprise awaits!

7

ANGOSTURA 7 YEAR OLD

Brand owner: Angostura Holdings
Website: www.angosturarum.com
Origin: Trinidad

HERE'S A SECOND EXPRESSION FROM ANGOSTURA IN TRINIDAD AND Tobago. This time we have their 7 Year Old style, aged in 'once used' bourbon casks until it is bottled. By the by, this is nothing unusual, as all former bourbon barrels are used just once. What would be exceptional would be a cask used twice for bourbon, as that would be illegal in the USA.

As we have learned, Angostura operate a modern five-column distillation plant, producing a lighter-bodied spirit in the modern style. Nothing wrong with that, especially once the rum has taken on a bit of age in a good quality cask. This particular premium rum is part of the International Collection, so don't look for it if holidaying on the islands, as a different range is offered locally. But if you do ever wash up there, you can visit the House of Angostura, located on a 20-acre complex in Trinidad, which, apart from its administration facility, includes a museum, art gallery, auditorium, merchandising shop, wine and spirits retail outlet, dining room and hospitality suites for visitors.

This rum is packed with mouth-watering flavours that include maple, chocolate, honey and tiramisu (or perhaps crème brûlée – I couldn't really make my mind up about that), presenting a warming taste that tapers slowly off to a sustained and satisfying conclusion.

It can be enjoyed as a sipping rum, neat or over ice, and equally it can mix a stunning contemporary take on a Manhattan or an Old Fashioned. And at well under £30 it's not at all bad value.

But if you've just won the National Lottery you could have fun tracking down one of the few remaining bottles of Angostura Legacy, released in 2012 to celebrate the fiftieth anniversary of Trinidad and Tobago as an independent nation. There were only 20 bottles (well, crystal decanters from Asprey, each with an elaborate sterling silver stopper) and they were released at $25,000 each, proudly proclaiming themselves 'the world's most expensive rum'.

While reading all about Trinidad and Tobago I learned that schoolchildren there are required to repeat their Independence Pledge at the beginning and end of term. Here's a little bit: 'I will be clean and honest in all my thoughts, my words and my deeds.' Nothing to do with Angostura rum, but I thought I'd share such a delightful and charming philosophy.

5

APPLETON ESTATE
JOY ANNIVERSARY

Brand owner: Gruppo Campari
Website: www.appletonestate.com
Origin: Jamaica

HOW GOOD CAN RUM BE? REALLY, REALLY GOOD – GREAT, IN FACT.
As great as this astonishingly fine 25-year-old blend from Jamaica's
Appleton Estate, bottled to commemorate Joy Spence's two decades
as Master Blender. Make no mistake, this is a world-class spirit.

So, here's my tip: before reading another word, get online and buy
some. They only made 1,200 bottles of this sublime nectar and it's
even been tipped as an investment. I don't hold with investing in
spirits, but I put this before you in the interests of full disclosure.
Don't blame me if it fails to soar in value, because then you can drink
it and give yourself a real treat. If you're quick and lucky, you may
find it for under £200.

Joy Spence is something of a legend in the distilling world, one of
the very few women in a senior position in rum and Appleton's first
female Master Blender. After 20 years at the top of her game, this
was released in early 2017 to mark her anniversary. She has plundered
the stocks of very old casks to bring us this aptly named Joy. It's a
blend of Appleton's finest aged casks – rums aged for between 25 and
35 years in Jamaica's Cockpit Country.

Appleton Estate is the country's oldest sugar estate and distillery in
continuous production; more than 265 years of distilling history in
the heart of an island soaked in rum. But despite the great age of the
components of the blend, it's still youthful and vibrant – joyful, in
fact.

DO NOT mix this. Joy is for sipping thoughtfully with good friends.
Joy may cause you to rethink your ideas about rum, it really is that
good. Joy is immensely rich and long-lasting; smack full of dark
orange, hints of a good Italian espresso coffee, Christmas cake and
dark brown sugar and, to be quite honest with you here, lots of other
good, tasty things that I can't quite manage to decode, so skilfully
have they been woven together. Like this tasting note, Joy's finish
goes on and on, generally the hallmark of true quality in spirits. Let
there be joy!

In fact, after a while, I gave up trying to write this entry and just sat
back and enjoyed this. You should follow my lead.

Well done, Joy. Here's to the next twenty years!

6

ATLÁNTICO PLATINO

Brand owner: Atlántico Importing Company
Website: www.atlanticorum.com
Origin: Dominican Republic

LET'S START WITH THIS NEWISH WHITE RUM FROM THE DOMINICAN
Republic (the larger part of the island once known as Hispaniola;
Haiti makes up the rest). The company is a venture by some former
Bacardí executives with connections to the island's sugar industry,
based around the southern city of La Romana, and supported by
investor and rum enthusiast Enrique Iglesias (a well known crooner).

It's a 100% sugar cane-based spirit, distilled locally in column stills,
then aged for around 12 months in American oak casks which
formerly contained bourbon and subsequently finished in barrels
that previously held Tempranillo wine. At that point, it has picked
up both flavour and colour from the wood, but it is then filtered to
remove the colour, giving its bright, clear presentation. Though at
first that may seem strange, it's not unusual in white rum production
and the key point is the richness of flavour delivered by this process.

The wood influence, particularly the American oak, is evident in
a rich vanilla nose, and the rum has a very smooth texture and
mouthfeel, suggestive of glycerine (just to be clear, I'm not suggesting
they add anything!). It is unusually smooth for white rum of this age
and, as such, could easily be drunk neat.

However, I think it's best as a mixer, such as in the time-tested Cuba
Libre (rum and Coke, as if you didn't know) or the classic Mojito.
The brand themselves suggest something called an 'Old Dominican',
which reads like a Mojito but substitutes a splash of champagne for
the conventional soda water. Well, I don't know about you, but in this
house we don't 'splash' champagne and if there's a bottle of bubbly on
the go it's savoured on its own. Though you could try it with cava, I
suppose . . .

Atlántico is a relatively recent arrival on these shores, and decent
value at £25–30 for the entry-level Platino. That's a little more than
the brand leader but it delivers more bang for your buck and the
sales do support, in part, a charitable foundation that has built local
schools. They also guarantee to source around a third of their sugar
cane from local farmers rather than giant agri-businesses, which is
decent of them.

Next up is their Gran Reserva, previously known as Private Cask.

7

ATLÁNTICO GRAN RESERVA

Brand owner: Atlántico Importing Company
Website: www.atlanticorum.com
Origin: Dominican Republic

THIS IS ATLÁNTICO'S TOP-OF-THE-LINE PREMIUM EXPRESSION.
I recently enjoyed drinking this until very early in the morning in the
company of my accountant. He had just checked my VAT return and
a serious, consolatory drink was called for!

However, a bottle of Atlántico Gran Reserva cheered us up
enormously and later the next day I felt better about everything. As
it happens, having been weaned on seriously heavy dark rums, the
accountant favours tackling rum with a drop of still water. Personally,
on that occasion, I went with a single ice cube, though I can see that
the water thing might work.

The Atlántico labels are quite good on transparency and inform
you that this is distilled from fresh cane juice and molasses and
aged in American whiskey barrels, with a refreshing absence of
spurious numbers with their suggestion of great age. Lurking in the
small print on the back label, however, are the dreaded words 'Mit
Farbstoff (Zuckerkulör) E150'.

You don't really want to see this. It's telling you that the final blend
has been treated with a small quantity of E150, a caramel-based
colouring agent produced by the heat treatment of sucrose, which is
used to give a uniform colour to the final product. Other producers
doubtless do this (it's more widespread than you realise in Scotch
whisky, especially in cheaper blends) but it only appears on labels
intended for the German market, as their legislation mandates that
the consumer be informed. While it's perfectly legal across the EU,
only the Germans insist on letting the customer know. Distillers
insist that E150 has no impact on flavour, but many critics would
disagree. Personally, I would rather it was left out on principle
and the glorious variability in colour of different batches of rum
celebrated and enjoyed, rather than obscured.

However, in the interests of full disclosure, I should add that I didn't
notice the slightly bitter edge that some maintain is associated with
E150 and nor did my accountant. The Gran Reserva is produced
using a solera system that blends rum made from fresh cane juice
(like the Platino) with some 'malta' (a weaker, more fully flavoured
sugar cane distillate and molasses-based rum, supplied in this
instance from a second Dominican distillery).

If your taste runs to a sweeter rum with notes of butter toffee,
caramel and maple syrup, then this will hit the spot.

8

BACARDÍ CARTA BLANCA

Brand owner: Bacardi and Company Ltd
Website: www3.bacardi.com
Origin: Puerto Rico

BECAUSE BACARDÍ ARE SO DOMINANT IN THE WORLD OF RUM, AND because many of us will have had our first taste of rum under the gaze of the bat, there's lots to say, so I'm going to spread this over four entries (bad luck if you're reading this sitting in the smallest room) and try to sum up the products at the end. Let's start with a rather self-serving disclosure, because Bacardí and I go back in time.

Some years ago now, Bacardí hired my then consulting company to design and subsequently project manage the construction of their Casa Bacardí brand home at their main distillery in San Juan, Puerto Rico. I think we made a pretty fine job of it. It's still there today and apparently attracting many visitors and making money for the company. But, in the way of these things, people moved on and we've rather lost touch. Today I concentrate on writing (though if you've got a chunky project, I could be persuaded to sharpen up my consultancy skills). I haven't worked for Bacardí for more than a decade, but I thought you should know that they once put food on my table. Quite a lot of tasty food, as it happens.

The San Juan distillery is enormous, as befits one of the biggest-selling spirits brands in the world, and Carta Blanca is how many of us experience rum for the first time. Some drinkers never move beyond this expression, and the received wisdom of the drinks industry is that Bacardí has 'transcended its category' – which is a long-winded way of saying that people simply ask for Bacardí, quite possibly not even realising it's rum. While the company hasn't had a completely trouble-free past few years, Bacardí is still a huge seller and a reference point for rum.

But let's step back into history. Bacardí, which remarkably remains family owned, was founded in 1862 in Santiago de Cuba when 47 year-old Spanish immigrant Don Facundo Bacardí Massó purchased a small distillery. He built on three great innovations that transformed Cuban rum: use of a standardised proprietary yeast, as opposed to reliance on wild yeasts; splitting his distillation into two runs to create greater complexity; and then charcoal filtering the barrel-aged rum to produce a lighter, clear spirit that was smooth to taste and appealing to look at.

But that's not all, so read on …

9

BACARDÍ CARTA ORO

Brand owner: Bacardi and Company Ltd
Website: www3.bacardi.com
Origin: Puerto Rico

DON FACUNDO WAS EVIDENTLY ONE SMART GUY AND A SHREWD businessman, who was quick to adopt his wife's suggestion of the iconic bat logo, but let's fast forward to the 1920s, when Prohibition in the USA gave Bacardí a huge boost. Cuba was a favourite holiday island for booze-deprived Americans and Bacardí exploited this, shrewdly (if bluntly) inviting their unfortunate neighbours to 'Come to Cuba and bathe in Bacardí rum.' And they did, in their thirsty tens of thousands, cementing Cuba's reputation for an easy-going and hedonistic party scene over the next two decades, during which time the company began a limited international expansion.

However, widespread political corruption followed the flood of tourist money and the steady growth of a Cuban revolutionary movement that was to find full expression in the 1950s. The Bacardí family initially supported Fidel Castro and the revolution, only to be bitterly disappointed by the new government's sudden confiscation of all their Cuban properties and bank holdings in October 1960. I can certainly see that coming as a disappointment.

Fortunately, the family had been hedging their bets. Prior to the communist takeover, ownership of the trademarks, assets and proprietary formulas had been discreetly relocated to the Bahamas. Distilleries had also been built in Mexico and Puerto Rico following Prohibition. The latter enjoyed favourable tax treatment on rum exported to the United States, where Bacardí was energetically and creatively marketed.

Consumer trends away from dark spirits in the 1960s and 70s also greatly assisted Bacardí, and this was a period of rapid growth, though senior family management also devoted much time, energy and money into fighting the Cuban regime and supporting exiled Cuban groups. Bacardí Carta Blanca built an impressive global position over these years and, by remaining in private family ownership, the company was well placed to expand from rum into other spirit categories.

Bacardí Oro dates from the earliest days of the company but was long known as Bacardí Gold, on account, as you can probably guess, of its golden colour. Keep going . . .

10

BACARDÍ CARTA NEGRA

Brand owner: Bacardi and Company Ltd
Website: www3.bacardi.com
Origin: Puerto Rico

THE LIGHTER BACARDÍ RUMS HAVE LONG BEEN ACKNOWLEDGED TO WORK well in cocktails, notably the Cuba Libre, Mojito, Daiquirí and the Ernest Hemingway Special. Cuban resident Hemingway was an enthusiastic consumer of Bacardí, but convinced he was diabetic and required a low sugar diet, he had this created for him at Havana's famous El Floridita bar and restaurant. Bacardí's association with cocktails resulted in several notable lawsuits in the USA, where the ingredients of a Bacardí Cocktail (a Daiquirí variant) are copyrighted – something the company jealously guards.

Growing interest in cocktails greatly benefited the company, especially in the USA where, from the late 1950s, the craze for tiki-style drinks put lighter rums in front of a mass market. Clever and sustained marketing, combined with Cuba's residual image as party central, established Bacardí as a brand virtually independent of the rest of the market. Later, Cuba came to have a furtive glamour as a kind of forbidden fruit, and even more recently, in a bid to provide the authenticity and heritage so earnestly sought after by millennials, Bacardí's marketing has emphasised its roots in Cuba, despite the fact that it has not distilled there for nearly 60 years. However, Bacardí has marketed a Havana Club brand in the USA since 1995, based on the original recipe created in Cuba in 1934 by fellow Cuban exiles and one-time distillers the Arechabala family. This has resulted in a complex dispute with Pernod Ricard and the Cuban government over the Havana Club trademark.

The Bacardí story is a long and complex one, which continues to this day. Wherever you stand on the taste of their rum, or in regard to the controversy attached to their marketing of a now somewhat faded Cuban provenance, their achievement is a remarkable one.

Distillation at the original Santiago distillery and its successor would have been using a pot still, but Cuban distillers were great innovators and rapidly adopted column still technology to create the lighter Cuban signature style that characterises Bacardí. Today their giant Puerto Rican distillery, known reverently as the 'Cathedral of Rum', works with molasses to produce batches of 40,000 gallons at a time. Rum is also aged here (and, I might just add, there's a very nice visitor centre). Further distilleries in Mexico, Spain and the Bahamas all produce Bacardí, officially identical in formula and process, though aficionados claim to be able to distinguish subtle differences.

11

BACARDÍ OCHO GRAN RESERVA (8 YEAR OLD)

Brand owner: Bacardi and Company Ltd
Website: www3.bacardi.com
Origin: Puerto Rico

Carta Blanca ('Bacardí'). This effectively defines the light white rum style. Designed for mixing, it's actually a more complex product than it first appears. Two distinct rum styles are separately aged for up to 24 months in ex-bourbon casks, then charcoal filtered and blended. Bottled at 37.5% for the UK, it's quite delicate, with subtle fruit and floral aromas. Most will be drunk with cola, which is fine if that's your taste, but it deserves more considered appreciation.

Carta Oro. Like the Carta Blanca, Oro is first aged then charcoal filtered, but retains a distinct gold colour. There's more to find here, as this complex blend is bottled at 40% and retains greater body and depth of flavour – the reason why it is widely seen as a house pour in many bars and restaurants. It may not excite the hardcore rum snob, but it will never disappoint.

Carta Negra. Also known as Bacardí Dark, this moves along the flavour spectrum and provides an unexpected twist on Bacardí. It was celebrated – somewhat to the discomfiture of the brand, I'd imagine – by rapper Eminem in his *Drug Ballad* (2000). How deeply, deeply unpleasant.

The rum itself carries up to four years of age and packs a bit more of a molasses punch. Sweet, rich and dark, this is Bacardí – but not as you know it.

Carta Ocho Gran Reserva. This is Bacardí getting serious and recognising that their previous line-up wasn't really cutting it with opinion-leading rum enthusiasts and top mixologists (who seem possessed of a somewhat limited attention span and appear to need constant variety). With premium rum on the march, Bacardí was not represented in this sector and so needed a powerful restatement of their rum credentials. This is a 40% blend (a little higher strength would have been nice) of rums aged for a minimum of eight years and some as long as 16.

At launch, it was said to have been the family's private reserve and was offered in very restricted quantities at $400. Today it's yours, sans ritzy decanter, for a considerably more modest £30 or less. At that price, just say 'Thank you, Señor Bacardí' and get your credit card out.

12

BALLY MILLÉSIME 2002

Brand owner: La Martiniquaise
Website: None
Origin: Martinique

HERE'S AN ABSOLUTELY CLASSIC AGED VINTAGE RUM IN THE RHUM agricole style. Bally have been releasing vintage dated rums since the 1920s (bottles do turn up from time to time but expect to pay four figures for such rarities). This 2002 vintage is the currently available expression, though you may find earlier releases. Incidentally, the company tell me that anything earlier than 1924 is certainly a fake. Watch out – there are counterfeiters out there looking to part you from your money.

This comes from another from the Bardinet company, part of the large French group La Martiniquaise, produced on the island of Martinique, where the company operated one of the first distilleries to distil rhum agricole from pure cane sugar. It has been granted the coveted Appellation Contrôlée status.

Bally are said to have a relatively slow style of maturation and certainly the spirit has gained depth and complexity before being bottled. But it is distinctively dry, so before splashing out the necessary 60-odd quid, be sure that you do like this style. If your taste runs to sweeter rums, this may not be your cup of tea.

The initial hit of sweetness on the nose flatters to deceive; it soon gives way to a more austere, spicy character with chocolate hints, some candied citrus peel and woody notes. It evolves to a complex finish – definitely one for slow sipping after a rich dinner.

M. Bally aimed originally for a style inspired by fine cognac and began the process of cask ageing in 1917, which I assume was somewhat radical for the period. In 1924, the first dated vintage was released, and the rum packaged in the characteristic rectangular bottles so reminiscent of a well-known brand of Scotch whisky. The packaging has hardly changed since then and thus retains a delightful retro look. Curiously, the authentic vintage style helps the bottle stand out from more recent competitors.

The original distillery closed in 1989 and was moved to Distillerie du Simon, where the rum is now produced. It's surely one for the connoisseur of this distinctive style, but a great benchmark, and an example of the remarkable value to be found in rum.

13

BALLY BLANC

Brand owner: La Martiniquaise
Website: None
Origin: Martinique

THIS IS THE WHITE VERSION OF BALLY'S RHUM AGRICOLE. I'VE featured some of the aged versions elsewhere, but it might be an idea to start with this one to give a wider appreciation of the style. It's very different from many of the sweeter Caribbean rums that we've grown used to here in the UK and it takes a moment or two of getting used to the dramatically different taste. You may find yourself asking if it's really rum. Well, for a large part of the world, it is.

Perseverance is called for then but go steadily because this is bottled at a tasty 50% strength. It's fresh, grassy and distinctively oily and rounded in the mouth. Like many in the rhum agricole style there are earthy notes somewhat reminiscent of the farmyard, but balanced with fruit (Poire William and overripe, sun-struck melon) and a slightly disconcerting saltiness on the finish. It's more complex and evolving than one might expect from a new-make spirit, bottled without any ageing.

As noted in the partner entries, this is from the Bardinet company, part of France's La Martiniquaise group, who are a major producer. The Bally range is well distributed in the UK, however, and it should be straightforward enough to find a bottle of this and also of the aged expressions in order to mount an interesting vertical tasting and experience the flavour evolution of a classic rhum agricole through barrel ageing.

Compare and contrast it too with St James Fleur de Canne.

Comparative tasting apart, this is probably best enjoyed in cocktails where its higher strength allows it to punch through the flavours of your chosen recipe. None of the range are particularly expensive and, at the time of writing, you should find this for around £30 a bottle – decent value when you take the extra strength into account.

In short, this is an honest-to-goodness classic of a particular style that gives a very decent account of itself once your palate has adapted to its distinctive delivery.

Deservedly popular in France, these Bally rums look set to become better known in the UK if rum continues to grow in popularity and drinkers become more and more discerning. It's certainly one to look out for and enjoy for its traditional merits and subtle pleasures.

14

BANKS 7 GOLDEN AGE BLEND

Brand owner: Bacardi and Company Ltd
Website: www.banksrum.com
Origin: Blend

ONCE UPON A TIME – 2008, IN FACT – AN EXPERIENCED AND well-connected drinks industry executive set up a boutique rum blending and bottling company called Banks. He claimed to have been inspired by the travels of eighteenth-century British explorer and botanist Sir Joseph Banks who, amongst the many achievements of his busy and fruitful life, sailed with the famous Captain Cook. That bit is true. You can please yourself if you buy the stuff about the inspiration for the brand.

However, the man so transcendentally captivated by this great and highly distinguished British scientist (though with no previously known connection of any significance to rum) was Arnaud de Trabuc, former CEO of Angostura Group and president of cognac producer Thomas Hine & Company, who had previously worked in the Caribbean.

Almost immediately, Banks was a modest success, selling Banks 5 Island Blend white rum and this Banks 7 Golden Age Blend (so called because it is made by blending 23 rums from eight distilleries from seven countries, namely Trinidad, Jamaica, Guyana, Barbados, Panama, Guatemala and Java) and a selection of limited edition bottlings under the Connoisseur's Cut label. Its reputation grew, especially on the US cocktail bar scene, and before long industry giants came calling. In July 2015, Banks was acquired by Bacardí, though you'd have to know the industry to be aware of that.

Why would the largest international rum brand in the world want to buy a boutique bottling house, especially now that they have their own premium styles and the even more expensive Facundo range? Well, basically, these big brands don't carry the cult appeal of small 'craft' operators to the opinion leaders in the bar trade, so they need (or feel they need) something to appeal to this rather fickle crowd. Bacardi have also bought a small bourbon distiller and a stake in a highly regarded independent bottler of Scotch whisky. Frankly, it's not a great deal of money to them, and is presumably worth it for the bragging rights while being considerably cheaper than developing their own small offshoot companies.

Banks 7 is very different in style to the Bacardi we're used to. Compared to most gold rums it's strikingly dry and full-bodied, one probably to drink neat over a little ice. As they say, 'Mixing won't improve our rum, but it should certainly improve your cocktail.'

15

BARBANCOURT 15 YEARS

Brand owner: D. Gardère & Cie
Website: www.barbancourt.net
Origin: Haiti

MANY YEARS AGO, I RECALL READING IN THE *FINANCIAL TIMES* (of all places) that Barbancourt was the best rum in the world. I don't hold with that type of simplistic and reductionist judgement, but if you were only going to try one of the rums listed here, well, this would be high on the list. I was torn between the eight and 15-year-olds for this listing, eventually picking the older of the two for no better reason than it's only a tenner more expensive than the younger version. You can pick up a bottle of this for under £50, which makes it one of the greatest bargains in the world of spirits.

It is quite legendary in rum-drinking circles, though – dare I say it – probably as much for its limited production and our lack of knowledge and understanding of Haiti as for its outstanding quality. The brand was founded in 1862 by Dupré Barbancourt, a French émigré from the Charente region. He began producing a high-class rum, which is now Haiti's best-known export. Today, the distillery remains in family hands, though it has relocated from the original site and increased production somewhat.

This is in spirit a rhum agricole, though not subject to the AOC rules that apply in Martinique. But for all that Haiti has been an independent state since 1804, the French influence remains strong and many commentators remark on a perceived resemblance to a fine cognac. The distillery themselves make a quite explicit connection, stressing on their website the importance that they attach to the double distillation method originating from Cognac.

This is certainly a complex and subtle product, demanding your careful attention and rewarding you accordingly. Look out for cooked pears, citrus fruits, cinnamon and pepper, all delivered with exceptional finesse and delicacy but without any loss of power.

If you like the taste, it may be worth stocking up with a few bottles. Haiti was struck by a powerful and devastating earthquake in January 2010. Tragically, two distillery workers were killed and more than 80 of them lost their houses. There was also damage to the ageing warehouses and a quantity of older stock was lost … well, you work it out.

A number of private label bottlings from the 1970s and 80s for the Italian market now appear at auction and are very collectable.

16

BARCELÓ IMPERIAL

Brand owner: Ron Barceló SRL
Website: www.ronbarcelo.com
Origin: Dominican Republic

THIS IS ONE OF SIX RUMS FROM THE DOMINICAN REPUBLIC IN MY 101, but it is probably better known in Spain, where it has long enjoyed considerable popularity.

The company was established in 1929 by one Julián Barceló but only began releasing rums under his name in 1950. The Imperial expression was launched in 1980 as a premium style. More recently, ownership has passed to a group of Spanish entrepreneurs and most of the company's efforts are directed to Spanish-speaking markets. Today the company only blends for its own brands and does not supply any third-party bottlers.

Imperial has won a number of notable awards though, if their website is to be believed, nothing since 2013. Perhaps they haven't entered any competitions in the last five years, or perhaps they need a new web manager . . . One can only speculate on the roots of such diffidence (kindly note that I resisted a mañana joke here).

Great stress is placed upon their adherence to the local Ron Dominicano quality standard, which guarantees compliance with the rum's denomination of origin. To meet this standard, the producers must harvest sugar cane and ferment, distill and age the alcohol in oak barrels for a minimum of one year, all in the territory of the Dominican Republic. Former bourbon barrels are used.

There are some reports that Barceló are planning their own distillery, though, as far as I can establish, for now they remain a blending and bottling operation, with the base spirit supplied from the large column stills of Alcoholes Finos Dominicanos, a specialist trade supplier of alcohol and related products. Barceló do, however, operate a large heritage centre which is open to visitors.

Though aged for a minimum of four years and styled as a premium expression – Imperial retails in the UK for around £30–35 – it is bottled at 38%, which is disappointing. Personally, I thought it drank rather thin and lacked substance or staying power. As a sub-£25 mixer it might work well, but the attractive bottle flatters to deceive and for my money there are better Dominican rums to be had, notwithstanding the awards and medals.

17

BAYOU SELECT

Brand owner: Louisiana Spirits LLC
Website: www.bayourum.com
Origin: USA

I TOOK ONE LOOK AT THIS AND KNEW – I JUST KNEW – THAT I WASN'T going to like it. There was something about the bottle and the label, with the grinning alligator and the 'Limited Edition Select Barrel Reserve' sticker that told me instinctively that this was going to be more about the sizzle than the sausage.

But, as they say in Lacassine, Louisiana, '*Laissez les bons temps rouler.*' As I am partial to some zydeco, I slipped my favourite Clifton Chenier into the CD player, cracked open the bottle and, as the great man got into his stride, things started to improve.

Yes, this is something of an upstart brand, from a distillery only founded in 2013 and already undergoing significant expansion, but folks have been making rum round that part of the world since the middle of the eighteenth century. Sugar cane grows well in the sultry climate and, with the strong French influence, distilling flourished and quantities of tafia (sugar cane spirit) were regularly shipped to Europe. However, the vagaries of the local industry were many and by the end of the last century the tradition was in danger of being completely lost or simply overtaken by bourbon.

Louisiana Spirits is a new company with a brand-new distillery but also with some very experienced distilling and blending staff who determined that, once again, world-class rum would be made from local sugar cane. Despite my scepticism about the bottle, I think they may be on to something because, even as the strains of Clifton's accordion hit my ears, the delicious, toasty aromas from the glass assailed my nostrils. There are both molasses and sugar in the base pot still distillates, combining both a Spanish and French approach to styles (the company's master blender was born in Cuba and trained in the Dominican Republic) and the final blend is passed through a solera system of both American oak (ex-bourbon) and French oak casks. The result is surprisingly mature, because the rums cannot be particularly old, yet it has depth and complexity.

It seems that others agree. The company make much of having collected 83 taste awards since they first released their rums, but I didn't need to know that to realise that my first impressions had let me down. The alligator has every reason for his cheeky smile on this great value drop of southern warmth.

18

BLACK TOT LAST CONSIGNMENT

Brand owner: Speciality Drinks Ltd
Website: www.blacktot.com
Origin: Guyana

I DON'T SUPPOSE THAT BACK ON 31 JULY 1970 ANYBODY ON BOARD one of the Royal Navy's ships imagined that the rum they were swallowing – quite possibly with a lump in their throat and a tear in their eye at the death of a great tradition and ritual – would ever command £1,500 a bottle. That's a serious chunk of change for any spirit, let alone the rum that had been given out every day since 1655 to sailors on board British naval vessels.

The rum ration was abolished on Black Tot Day: 'The Admiralty Board concludes that the rum issue is no longer compatible with the high standards of efficiency required now that the individual's tasks in ships are concerned with complex, and often delicate, machinery and systems on the correct functioning of which people's lives may depend.' The lives of bad people we want to kill, that is.

And that was that. Except that it wasn't. There was quite a lot of rum left, which languished in storage for some years before the remaining stock was bought by the entrepreneurially minded chaps at The Whisky Exchange (that's the consumer-facing part of Speciality Drinks Ltd) and bottled in 2010 as Last Consignment (54.3%; £650). It was a blend of rums from the last consignment produced for the Navy, stored in flagons for decades before its blending and rebirth. This is hardcore dark rum, packed with molasses, treacle, muscovado sugar, roasted nuts and hints of balsamic vinegar.

Then, more recently, the luxury Black Tot 40 Year Old (44.4%; £1,500) expression was launched. This was actually distilled some five years after Black Tot Day, so is more of a tribute to the spirit of the original than part of the actual Royal Navy stock, but still a remarkable achievement in its own right – not least for surviving 40 years in wood in Guyana, where this was distilled.

Like the earlier release, this is a rum that's not to be trifled with. Or, indeed, to make trifle with. Take this slowly, very slowly, for this is liquid history.

If you don't want to pay £1,500 and have a home for a few gallons of the original rum, then flagons of the Royal Navy issue in their traditional wicker caskets do turn up from time to time in online auctions. 'Up spirits!'

19

BLACKWELL BLACK GOLD

Brand owner: Well Black Spirits LLC
Website: www.blackwellrum.com
Origin: Jamaica

THIS IS OLD HARROVIAN CHRIS BLACKWELL'S LOVE NOTE TO JAMAICA, where this remarkable man of many talents has spent much of his life. Born in 1937, he is related to the Crosse & Blackwell family and, on his mother's side, to the Appleton and J. Wray & Nephew rum distilling dynasties.

He worked on the classic Bond movie *Dr. No* and, still only 21, founded Island Records, introducing ska and reggae to the world. The highly influential label launched the careers of a number of international music artists in the 1970s and 80s – too many to mention, though he did apparently turn down Elton John. Oh, and he bought Ian Fleming's house Goldeneye, which is now just one of the upmarket resorts he owns on the island.

What a guy! That's quite enough for one life, you'd think. But in 2009 he turned to his distilling roots and released this Black Gold rum. We don't know if his mother helped (she lived to the age of 104, passing away in August 2017) but it's said to be based on a traditional recipe from the days when her family dominated Jamaican distilling. So, naturally, it's distilled on Jamaica, by J. Wray & Nephew, and is a blend using a traditional heavy pot and a lighter column still rum. Once distilled, it is aged in American oak barrels, and the renowned Joy Spence is said to have had a hand in the blending. Everyone concerned is a little coy about the exact age though.

I don't think it matters. For less than £20, this stuff is a steal and it's nice to know that every sale generates a contribution to Island ACTS, a Jamaican community charity. If I had one minor quibble, it would be with the label, styled to look like a pirate map. With this rum's credentials, it really doesn't need such a clichéd gimmick, and though the presentation (designed by Blackwell's business partner, ad man 'Madboy' Richard Kirshenbaum) is said to suggest this is a 'drink with attitude', that all feels rather childish. Still, it probably reflects where rum saw itself in 2009, which only goes to show how far it has come.

Naturally, it goes down a storm in cocktails and the website offers a number of suggestions along with, predictably enough, a very funky soundtrack. You'll be shaken and stirred (we'll credit that to *Dr. No* – see what I did there?).

20

BOTRAN SOLERA 1893

Brand owner: Industrias Licoreras de Guatemala
Website: www.botranrums.com
Origin: Guatemala

SPICY, SWEET BUTTERSCOTCH ROLLS GENTLY OFF THE AROMA OF THIS Guatemalan rum just as soon as the cork is pulled, as if it's anxious to jump into your glass. And then there's more to find, as spice and cut cigar notes develop on the palate and a lingering, biscuity finish unwinds more than agreeably as you contemplate another glass. It's that kind of rum – easy drinking, without lacking complexity or weight, and I'd defy anyone not to enjoy this as a sipping rum: it's simply too good to be swamped in a cocktail.

The history of aged rums in Guatemala is strongly linked to the Botrans, one of the founding families of Industrias Licoreras de Guatemala (they were also the force behind Zacapa, assuming you read as far as the letter Z – spoiler alert: it's at the end of the book).

In the mid twentieth century, five brothers of the Botran family from Burgos, Spain settled in Guatemala. Over time, this family succeeded in perfecting the art of rum production through the combination of old European traditions, such as the solera ageing system, with the use of local resources, such as crystal-clear mountain water, specific kinds of sugar cane and some innovative processes to obtain concentrated sugar cane juice.

Life begins for this rum at the Tululá sugar mill, located on the south coast of Guatemala, where climate, topography, and soil characteristics create the conditions to grow late-maturing sugar cane varieties that are highly valued for their sugar concentrations. Contrary to what you may read on the web, Botran uses only sugar cane, not molasses, and employs a proprietary yeast derived from pineapple leaves. Fermentation is unusually long, at 120 hours, increasing the complexity of the base spirit.

The various rums then enter the Botran solera system and, in the case of this Solera 1893 expression, are aged some 2,400 meters above sea level in American white oak barrels, new and charred, that previously held American whiskey, then in old sherry casks and finally finished in port barrels over a period of 18 years.

For this complexity, obsessive care and long-term family commitment you'll be asked the princely sum of around £40. Doesn't seem so bad, does it? But, please, just don't go splashing cola in it. They've a Reserva Blanca for that. If you must.

21

BOUKMAN

Brand owner: Boukman Rhum, LLC
Website: www.boukmanrhum.com
Origin: Haiti

'BOTANICAL' RUM FROM HAITI – WHAT'S THAT ABOUT? BASICALLY, this is traditional Haitian artisanal spiced rhum, to a considerable degree unchanged for centuries, now exposed to some sophisticated marketing and packaging expertise and fast-forwarded to the twenty-first century by an experienced drinks trade manager with a background in new product development.

Looking at the funky packaging you could be forgiven for mistaking this for the very latest small-batch craft gin. Add a knock-out bottle to that 'Botanical' labelling and the knowledge that the distillate is infused with Haitian native woods, barks, bitter orange peel, allspice, clove, vanilla, bitter almond and cinnamon and the resemblance to gin becomes uncannily close.

But it's not. This is the authentic taste of spiced rhum agricole or clairin trempè, distilled from fresh sugar cane juice then infused to create some unexpected flavours. The spirit itself comes from two of Haiti's best rhum terroirs, the rich cane fields of Croix-des-Bouquets in the south and the northern cane fields around Cap-Haïtien, scene of Dutty Boukman's rebellion.

Who? Well, he was the Haitian slave and vodou priest who was an early and influential leader of the famous slave revolt of 1791. Though Boukman was killed, the rebellion could not be denied. It led to Haiti's independence and the establishment of the first nation state free from slavery, ruled by non-whites and former captives. Fittingly, his rousing call to freedom is quoted on a little panel on the label.

Things haven't gone so well for Haiti in recent times, but products like Boukman come with a social conscience. Company founder Adrian Keogh donates a share of profits to charitable programmes that help the sugar cane communities and to Haiti Futur, which is transforming education in Haiti with modern technology.

So, funky packaging, great backstory, community engagement and intriguing product. But is it any good? Well, yes, it is. I'd go so far as to say it's the most interesting new spirit I've seen in quite some time. Drunk neat, over a little ice, it's genuinely very enjoyable with fascinating and unusual flavour notes at every turn.

Put it this way: buy this and you have the coolest Rum Top Trumps card ever!

22

BRISTOL BLACK SPICED

Brand owner: Bristol Spirits Ltd
Website: www.bristolclassicrum.com
Origin: Blend

THERE ARE SPICED RUMS, GOOD SPICED RUMS, TASTY SPICED RUMS and then there is this, the apotheosis of spiced rum, a veritable Mount Parnassus of poetry, music and learning in a bottle. Or, to put it another way, I quite like it.

Of course, I really want to write about the various one-off limited bottlings from this small independent West Country merchant, who specialise in hard-to-find stellar rums that are near impossible to source elsewhere. Right now they are offering rums from Haiti, Grenada, Cuba, Peru and Mauritius amongst others that sound lip-smackingly good as well as rum from legendary distilleries such as Caroni and Port Morant – but as any one of these could run out at any moment, I shan't mention them. Doesn't stop you taking a quick peek, though, does it?

Instead, if you like spiced rum, fill your boots with Bristol Black Spiced and all shall be well in your world. And if you don't like spiced rum then buy some anyway and change your mind.

As the label says, it reflects the rich and varied history of this marvellously diverse city with its tobacco merchants, rum shippers, sugar barons, canal and railway engineers, explorers, fisherfolk and so on. Curiously, though, they don't mention Bristol's infamous slave trade. Bristol is now home to the *SS Great Britain*, and if you want a spurious pirate connection to rum, then the infamous Captain Blackbeard (inspiration, some do say, for the *Pirates of the Caribbean* movies) was born here. There are even pirate tours of the old docks led by Pirate Pete himself. (Just my wild guess, but he's probably not a real pirate, but he has a skull and crossbones hat – what more do you expect for a tenner?)

Now, the foregoing is not merely flippant filler. [*Could have fooled me. Ed*] I merely wanted to convey the sense that this remarkable product itself conveys a sense of its home town in a most unusual way. It's a blend of aged rums, origin unspecified, with generous helpings of fruit and spice. Thankfully it is far from sweet, compared to the spiced rum you may be thinking of, more resembling a liquid Christmas cake with marzipan and dark, brooding, spicy depths. You could actually use it in your Christmas cake, splash some onto a traditional plum pudding or give some to gran instead of the usual sherry.

Or, on second thoughts, just keep it for yourself.

23

BRUGAL 1888 RON GRAN RESERVA FAMILIAR

Brand owner: Edrington Group
Website: www.brugal-rum.com
Origin: Dominican Republic

EDRINGTON IS A NAME MORE FAMILIAR TO SCOTCH WHISKY DRINKERS: they own The Macallan and Highland Park single malts and The Famous Grouse and Cutty Sark blends amongst other things. As a minor curiosity, the ultimate holding entity is a charitable trust and, eventually, the company's profits are disbursed to worthy causes, mainly in Scotland.

Some years ago, they embarked on a strategy of widening their portfolio and in February 2008 bought a substantial majority share of Brugal, a long-established, family-owned distiller in the Dominican Republic. Not that you would know that from the Brugal website, which merely refers coyly to an 'association' with Edrington.

At that time, the belief was that global sales of rum were about to increase rapidly, and rum would broaden the Edrington portfolio. Of course, what no one anticipated was that a global financial crisis was about to set back the world economy by at least five years (and many would say that the effects have yet to be fully worked out). So, this acquisition hasn't been the rip-roaring success that the canny Scots accountants who head the Edrington Group anticipated, but it may yet prove a shrewd move despite significant write-downs in Brugal's book value in 2013 and 2015.

What can't be debated is the underlying quality of the Brugal heritage and the range of rums produced by the two Brugal family Maestra Roneras who remain in charge of making and blending the rums. Today, a tightly focused selection is offered to the UK market, and this Brugal 1888 Ron Gran Reserva Familiar is something of a showpiece. Informed opinion suggests that while Edrington have – wisely – not interfered in the distillation process, they have brought some of their renowned expertise in wood selection and cask management to the table, with some success.

This is well seen here. The rum spends up to eight years in former bourbon barrels but is then transferred to first-fill Spanish oak casks, something of an Edrington speciality. The result is a pleasantly dry and lively palate on a rum that opens in a rather delicate and restrained manner, continuing to grow and evolve as the various layers of flavour become apparent. If you want a sweeter rum, ignore this, but for elegance and balance Brugal is hard to fault.

24

BUMBU

Brand owner: Bumbu Rum Company
Website: www.bumbu.com
Origin: Barbados

THE FIRST THING THAT STRIKES YOU ABOUT THIS DISTINCTIVELY packaged spiced rum is, well, the distinctive packaging. Someone has gone to a lot of trouble here: the glass is reassuringly heavy and crystal clear; the striking logo cleverly references the crossed bones of the pirate flag and the 'X marks the spot' of the treasure maps of fiction; the Bumbu name and the X device is embossed on the glass; and finally there is a real cork stopper, with the X making a third appearance.

On opening the bottle, there was the satisfying noise of a drawn cork and then a very pervasive aroma of ripe bananas and vanilla filled the room. So, my first thought was that the blender might have gone a bit far with the added spices. The claim is that it is 'based on' recipes used by sixteenth and seventeenth-century sailors who, it is said, 'blended native Caribbean ingredients into their rum and called it "Bumbu"'. Gilding the lily, the brand then suggests that this is 'truly the original craft spirit'.

I beg to differ. I'm not sure that sixteenth and seventeenth-century sailors were all that particular about the spices they mixed into their grog, and even if they were, I doubt that they were overly meticulous in recording the details. And, not to be pedantic, but the continuous column stills where the base rum is distilled, do not constitute a craft distillery. Finally, at least in the UK, this is bottled at 35% ABV which means it is legally a 'Spirit Drink'. To be fair, it doesn't claim to be rum, though you might easily jump to that conclusion.

However, forget all that: the last paragraph is really for the purists, who won't like Bumbu at all. It's too sweet, too accessible and too transparently a marketing construct to satisfy their fastidious tastes. So why include it?

Well, because Bumbu is doing well on the club scene. Served by the bottle with an ice bucket jammed with mixers, it's the type of product drunk to the accompaniment of pounding garage or drill music (kindly excuse these genre references - my sorry attempt to get down with da yuff). It's a contemporary expression of where many rums see themselves and a gateway product that may tempt some drinkers to explore further. As such, it's the future (or part of it) and deserves its place. Sorry, purists.

25

BUNDABERG
EXPORT STRENGTH

Brand owner: Diageo
Website: www.bundabergrum.com.au
Origin: Australia

THEY DRINK LOTS OF THIS IN THAT LAND DOWN UNDER, WHERE women glow and men plunder (note the clever reference there to Men At Work's 1981 hit '*Down Under*'), or Terra Australis, as the explorer Matthew Flinders might have said. Can you tell what it is yet?

Yes, here we have the confusingly labelled Export Strength Underproof Rum from Bundaberg, Australia's most famous export after Vegemite and second-hand VW camper vans. It's 'Export Strength' because it's 40%, as opposed to the 37% stuff they get away with domestically, and 'Underproof' because, well, it really ought to be stronger. It also has a polar bear on the label, a distant cousin of the koala.[3]

Polar Bears are cool. Not as cool as Paddington, though.

They've actually been making rum here since 1889. It's been a huge success in its home market since the earliest days (despite the odd setback, such as a distillery fire, but that's almost mandatory in any good distillery story). In 2000 it was bought by Diageo, though their international marketing favours Captain Morgan and Zacapa.

Originally the aim was to use the waste molasses from the local sugar mills and the distillery was financed by a consortium of local businessmen with interests in sugar. Molasses – a rather alarming four Olympic-sized swimming pools of the stuff every year – remain the feedstock for Bundaberg, who use a mixture of column and pot stills for their various rums.

And, as well as this Export Strength, they do actually make quite a few, though the better ones are quite rare here – about as rare as a polar bear in the Outback, in fact. Still, 'Bundy' is a great favourite amongst Aussies who love its highly distinctive taste.

As you might anticipate from its origin, it's an honest-to-goodness, plain-speaking, direct sort of a cobber with few airs and graces. There's nothing wrong with that, but this is probably best enjoyed with a decent ginger ale or cola (Bundaberg apparently make their own) and a generous handful of ice. I could see it going down well at the Gabba to the merry sound of English wickets tumbling at regular intervals (another Aussie soundtrack there for you).

---

3   In case you haven't guessed, I made that up.

26

CADENHEAD'S CLASSIC

Brand owner: J. & A. Mitchell
Website: www.wmcadenhead.com
Origin: Guyana

IT'S NOT REALLY POSSIBLE TO WRITE ABOUT RUM WITHOUT SOME mention of the merchant and bottler William Cadenhead's. Established in 1842, they are Scotland's oldest firm of this type, today controlled by J. & A. Mitchell, the same private owners behind the legendary Springbank distillery.

They acquired the business when it ran into difficulties in 1972. By that point, all the stock had been sold at auction - said to be the largest sale of wines and spirits ever held in Great Britain – and though Mitchell's bought the name, goodwill and original shop, there was much to do to rebuild the firm.

By concentrating on single malt whiskies and fine rum and never chill filtering or colouring their releases, a reputation was built up amongst connoisseurs and enthusiasts who appreciated this approach, unfashionable though it was at the time. The shops still present a somewhat antediluvian appearance, but do not be fooled: the people behind the counter know and love their products and approach their job with real enthusiasm. 'By test the best' wrote an early proprietor, and this remains the firm's motto to this day. They are not funky, but they enjoy the highest of reputations amongst those 'in the know' and have now built up a small chain of shops in the UK and on the Continent.

Several of their private bottlings have achieved very high marks in independent tastings and they have a remarkable range of single distillery, single cask rum bottlings. Do not let looks deceive you: modest and unassuming they may be, particularly in contrast to today's elaborate presentations, these are stellar rums, upon which an unrivalled reputation has been built. Oh, and they do some pretty decent whiskies as well.

In style and approach then, Cadenhead's stand almost alone. You could do much worse than starting with their Classic Rum. It is, as it says, 'classic' – rich, packed with dried fruits and archetypal Demerara notes, warming and full-flavoured. It's everything you might want in a Caribbean rum and great value when you take the 50% strength into account. They say that the latest release 'blew us away' when they were tasting and I can well believe it.

Grab some of this and enjoy old-fashioned quality and value.

27

CARGO CULT SPICED RUM

Brand owner: The Small Batch Spirits Company
Website: www.cargocultrum.com.au
Origin: Blend

ON ORIGINALLY VISITING THE ISLAND OF TANNA, HRH PRINCE PHILIP, Duke of Edinburgh was greeted as a deity.

This was not, I'll admit, the first thing I expected I'd be researching when I agreed to write a book on rum. But the good people of Yaohnanen on Tanna (it's in remote Vanuatu), earnest followers of the Prince Philip Movement, still hold that His Royal Highness descended from one of their spirit ancestors. You never know; stranger things have happened…

The Prince Philip Movement is a modern cargo cult. The story of the cargo cults of the Pacific islands has long intrigued me, leading me to include this particular spiced rum, which celebrates the John Frum cult, also from Vanuatu. John Frum is said to be a corruption of 'John from . . .' and refers to the impact of US service personnel arriving on these remote islands during WW2 with supplies and technologies that were seen by the islanders as magical gifts from the gods.

After the troops departed, the islanders constructed airstrips and built replica planes in the belief that the 'gods' would return with more wonderous goods. *Post hoc, ergo propter hoc*, we might conclude.

The cargo cult is a logical fallacy and, let's face it, you didn't expect to find *that* in a rum book. There were actually cargo cults long before WW2, first recorded in fact in Fiji in 1885. Which is a nice link, as Cargo Cult comprises rums from Fiji and Papua New Guinea that are blended and spiced in Australia. It's a tasty little drop and surprisingly dry – there's no added sugar, the curse of some spiced rums, but heaps of spicy fruit cake and notes of cinnamon, cloves and dried oranges.

My one major criticism is the 38.5% strength, which means it drinks a little thin when tried neat. However, you'll likely be mixing this: the website lists all manner of cocktails and suggests serving Cargo Cult with cola, freshly opened coconut milk, ginger ale (which works well) or pineapple and ginger ale (I liked that even more). But you could well quibble at paying more than £30, especially having noted the lower-than-normal strength, so it would be a kindness to us mortals if the Cargo Cult gods could get this down a little bit.

Might a prayer to the Duke of Edinburgh help?

28

CHALONG BAY FINE SPIRIT

Brand owner: Andaman Distillers Co., Ltd
Website: www.chalongbayrum.com
Origin: Thailand

CHALONG BAY — THE 'SPIRIT OF PHUKET', OR SO THEY INSIST — WAS established in 2013 by two French entrepreneurs, Marine Lucchini and Thibault Spithakis, using locally grown sugar cane and, naturally, French distillation methods. They observed that the cultivation of sugar cane originated in South East Asia (probably in New Guinea, circa 8,000 BC says Wikipedia) long before it was taken to the West Indies, something we can put down to the first Spanish and Portuguese explorers, and that the local crop was not being exploited for spirits production.

Noting also Phuket's tourist industry and the large number of younger travellers, they also added a cocktail workshop and a bar to the Chalong Bay offer. Judging by web reviews and social media this has proved a considerable success. It scores well on TripAdvisor; no surprise really.

The Chalong Bay Fine Spirit – not technically a rum, but a Spirit Drink – divides opinion, however. It's very much in the rhum agricole tradition and, as the business is very new, there are as yet no aged expressions available, though there are a range of five flavoured infusions. Much emphasis is placed on cocktails.

Based on my admittedly limited sampling of the Fine Spirit product, this is probably wise. Tasted neat, it is in my opinion reminiscent of low-grade rubbing alcohol or, in the words of one online review 'only good for domestic cleaner'. Actually, I think my fastidious and discrimating cleaner would, quite understandably, leave if served this.

I suspect this is one of those products that tastes great on holiday, but is discovered upon return to have travelled poorly, migrating to the back of the drinks cupboard until eventually being served to very drunk neighbours at New Year, used in an attempt to light the barbeque or simply tipped away. If any of my neighbours are reading this, please be assured it will never be offered under my roof.

But others love it and occasionally I caught a pleasantly fruity aroma on the nose. As ever, my conclusion is that you have to make up your own mind.

Top tip: try to get it at the domestic price of around 650 Thai baht (under £15) and then you won't feel quite as bad about it.

29

CHAMAREL XO

Brand owner: La Rhumerie de Chamarel
Website: www.rhumeriedechamarel.com
Origin: Mauritius

IF, FOR SOME ESOTERIC REASON OF YOUR OWN (AND I WON'T PRY), you determined to get to Western Australia from Madagascar by boat, you'd likely put in to the island of Mauritius. It's in the Indian Ocean, around 1,100 kilometres away (a bit less than the distance from Land's End to John o' Groats, if that helps).

And that would be your great good fortune, because fine rum in the French style is distilled on Mauritius. Amongst the distilleries there is La Rhumerie de Chamarel which, if its website can be relied upon, has a jolly fine restaurant and, after a few days' hard sailing, you'd probably welcome some decent grub. I'd like to offer a personal endorsement but regrettably my publisher declined to fund the necessary research trip.

I can, however, draw your attention to their extensive range of rums, all produced from sugar cane grown on the surrounding eco-friendly estate, where vast plantations of sugar cane grow side by side with pineapples and other tropical fruits (sounds fantastic – do they do press trips, I wonder?). The estate was first established in the 1790s by Charles-Antoine de Chazal de Chamarel, whose family managed it for many, many years.

It was sold in 1996 to another family, who remain discreetly anonymous (though according to *Lonely Planet*, they may be the owners of the Beachcomber chain of luxury hotels). The state-of-the-art distillery and visitor centre was opened in 2008, and has subsequently been expanded.

Since then, they have slowly been building an international reputation, with a range of blanc and aged rums and some liquors. Whoever owns the business, they either know what they're doing or have hired some experienced people. The XO is pure cane rhum agricole, part distilled in a column still and part in a pot still (30%). Each is aged separately for six to eight years in a unique combination of French oak barrels – new ones, ex-cognac and ex-wine, re-charred – giving notes of vanilla, smooth oak, orange, pepper and clove. With plenty of fruit on the palate it leads nonetheless to an agreeably dry finish and, even at 43%, this is a most agreeable sipping rum in an elegantly presented bottle.

Apparently, the XO is a great family favourite so, whoever they are, they have great taste.

30

COR COR GREEN

Brand owner: Grace Rum Company Ltd
Website: www.gracerum.sakura.ne.jp
Origin: Japan

ONE OF THE GREAT JOYS ABOUT THIS RUM JOURNEY IS FINDING unexpected rums in unexpected places – such as Minami-daitō-jima (once known as South Borodino island), one of the Daitō Islands, situated off the south-east coast of Okinawa, Japan.

Cor Cor Green was the brainchild of founder Ms Yuko Kinjo, who noted the apparent similarities of the island groups of her native Okinawa Prefecture with those of the Caribbean. Not slavery and piracy, but sugar production, which had flourished since the island was first settled in the early part of the twentieth century.

Okinawa is noted in history, of course, for its blood-stained part in the Second World War but otherwise has made little impact on the West. Sugar cane was grown and processed there but it was not until 2002 that the entrepreneurial Ms Kinjo partnered with the local Chamber of Commerce to get into the rum business.

Three styles are produced: Red uses molasses, Premium is an aged variant (I've been unable to determine how old), but, interesting as these are, what really caught my eye was the Green, which is made in the French agricole style from the fermented juice of freshly squeezed sugar cane. In this, it is similar to the other Japanese rum listed here, Ryoma (entry 83).

Like Ryoma, it's simply packaged but, to be honest, not terribly cheap. Japan is hardly a low-cost economy, and this has come a long way and it is a true small-batch, artisanal product from small pot stills, so perhaps it is to be expected.

The rum itself is quite intense with pronounced vanilla notes and, as an exotic example of the agricole style, possibly one for the connoisseur or enthusiastic seeker of curiosities (I'm being tactful, you'll appreciate) rather than rum neophytes. The distillery's publicity material describes it as 'vibrant and strong', stating bluntly that, 'We'll be the first to admit that our rums are not for everyone'.

Well, fair enough. Not everyone likes kippers, or Marmite (I don't), or ripe Stilton (I do), or real ale. Life would be most terribly monotonous if we all liked the same things or didn't try new things. Be warned, therefore, but don't hold back unduly. Who knows what you might miss.

31

CRUZAN SINGLE BARREL

Brand owner: Beam Suntory
Website: www.cruzanrum.com
Origin: St Croix, US Virgin Islands

I APPROACHED THIS WITH SOME CONSIDERABLE ANTICIPATION. AFTER all, it's not every day that you find a 'single barrel' expression of any spirit for around £30, so it seemed like quite the bargain.

And, indeed, for £30 it is, but it's not quite the bargain it seems if you take the 'single barrel' terminology at face value. What actually happens here is that rums of between five and 12 years of age are blended and then popped back into different barrels for further ageing of around a year and then bottled 'one cask at a time'. So, if your reference point is Scotch, what we have here is a Barrel Finish, or some such.

Actually, it's probably a Jim Beam Bourbon Cask finish, as I'm given to understand that the majority of casks come from that world-famous bourbon, also part of the same group, where they have been used only once and retain plenty of life, along with the influence of the previous occupant.

But while you may think that owners Beam Suntory (probably better known for their whiskies, which include Jim Beam, Maker's Mark, Yamazaki and Laphroaig) have played a little fast and loose with the description, the rum itself has been thrilling critics, with a pleasing pile of plaudits to justify their claim to be the world's most honoured rum distillery – though Bacardí might cough at that and even Bumbu make a similar claim.

It's located on the island of St Croix in the US Virgin Islands which, to the understandable chagrin of other Caribbean producers, enjoys a benevolent tax regime. Perhaps for this reason, Cruzan is seen more frequently in the USA than here in Europe.

Despite being in the ownership of a giant corporation, Cruzan (the name is derived from 'Crucian' – a native of St Croix) is managed by the seventh generation of the Nelthropp family, who have a connection to sugar planting and rum here dating back to 1760. However, it is many years since local sugar plantations supplied the distillery and today it runs its sophisticated five-column still set-up on molasses imported from Guatemala.

The result is a rum that is relatively light-bodied but not lacking in complexity, and well suited to mixing. If you like such things, Cruzan also produce a huge range of flavoured rums, some of which sound perfectly vile (Blueberry Lemonade, anyone?).

32

DARK MATTER

Brand owner: Dark Matter Distillers
Website: www.darkmatterdistillers.com
Origin: Scotland

WELL, THIS IS DIFFERENT. FROM BOTTLE TO LABEL TO WEBSITE AND above all to taste, this is certainly different.

Oh, and it's distilled in Scotland, so that's different as well. Dark Matter are based in darkest Aberdeenshire and began distilling their rum – from molasses, naturally – in April 2015, thus predating Orkney's VS Distillers with their J. Gow Spiced by two years.

Dark Matter Spiced Rum has certainly divided opinion on forums, and it's powerful stuff. Packed with more spices than the average wholefood shop, the nose is intense, the palate is intense and the finish, well, very long and intense. This is the vindaloo of spiced rums, so if you like loads of ginger, cloves, peppercorns and allspice berries you're going to love this.

On the other hand, if you don't, you'll join the chorus of criticism on retailer sites. 'Vile' wrote one reviewer, adding 'Hands down [to] the most disgusting drink I've had the misfortune to ever have'. 'Tastes like it is intended as some kind of joke shot drunk only as student dares.' The critic was not alone, but while there were a few more comments in a similar vein, it's fair to record a decent number of very positive scores as well. No one marked it with two or three stars – this is a love it or hate it product which has collected awards in blind tastings. Make of that what you will.

Let's note that it is distilled in Scotland by two brothers who are new to the distilling trade, having worked previously in the oil industry. They've invested in professional equipment and seem set for the long term, aiming to launch a white rum as well as this spiced variant. To their credit, they are quite transparent about the recipe for the spice infusion and candidly admit to a high degree of post-distillation dosing with sugar.

Sadly, the website, which I thought rather self-consciously funky, doesn't really enlighten the visitor. There is a certain amount of important looking science-speak that, despite sounding significant, doesn't seem to add up to very much. That's a shame, because this is an innovative venture and I'm all for a few provocative pioneers stirring things up a bit.

In physics, dark matter is a hypothetical construct, never directly observed. This particular Dark Matter, however, delightful though it would be from a hip flask on a sharp winter's day, strikes me as more of a spiced ginger liqueur. Tasty, though.

33

DEADHEAD

Brand owner: Iconic Brands, Inc.
Website: www.deadheadrum.com
Origin: Mexico

IF YOU'VE SEEN CRYSTAL HEAD VODKA AND DI GIN, YOU'LL KNOW that there's been something of a fashion in recent years in the spirits industry for ever more outré packaging – that's outré as in weird, outlandish, offbeat, far out, freakish, grotesque, quirky, zany, eccentric, off-centre, idiosyncratic and unconventional, not to say downright ludicrous or preposterous.

This is all of those things, which I suppose is the point. It certainly will stand out on a shelf, though the question is whether you find the idea of drinking rum served from a shrunken head appealing (not a real one, by the way – no actual heads were harmed in the making of these bottles).

It's the creation of one Kim Brandi, founder and CEO of Iconic Brands, and colleagues, who are also responsible for some other questionably packaged tequilas. They're American, of course. But let's not argue with success – Deadhead has been growing rapidly since its launch and for a small independent company has turned in some impressive numbers in the highly competitive spirits business. Competitive and, in the USA at least, highly litigious – Brandi is no stranger to copyright and other lawsuits it seems.

The rum itself is a six-year-old Mexican blend of pot and column still rums, from both sugar cane and molasses, produced today at the 65-year-old family-controlled Destilados Bonampak distillery, run by Cuban rum veterans. Apart from that, there's little that I can tell you about this, other than it will cost you more than £50, which feels rather a lot, though the cap can serve as a shot glass if that helps at all. I quite liked the rum, which was pleasant enough. After a glass or two I could feel it going to my head (sorry).

But while the rum is Mexican, the packaging is said to be inspired by the Amazonian Shuar people. Why? Well, because apparently they have maintained the tradition of shrunken heads, taken from their enemies as war trophies. And if that wasn't enough of a cultural ragbag, the website proudly displays a sign reading 'ALOHA', which is a Hawaiian greeting of love, affection and peace, and another reading 'FUCK OFF' which is an Anglo-Saxon greeting conveying, well, quite the opposite.

So, at that point, not wanting to lose my head, off I jolly well fucked.

34

DEPAZ BLANC CUVÉE DE LA MONTAGNE

Brand owner: La Martiniquaise
Website: www.depazrhum.com
Origin: Martinique

HERE'S A VERY GOOD PLACE TO START IF YOU WANT TO UNDERSTAND the distinctively French agricole style.

Now, you wouldn't imagine that very much good could come out of a volcanic eruption that killed more than 30,000 people, but the 1902 eruption of Mount Pelée on Martinique, which destroyed the Depaz estate and chateau along with much of the island's capital city, left behind the legacy of a rich volcanic soil that proved perfect for growing blue cane sugar. This rare variety, difficult to grow, produces the highest and best yield of sugar for the production of rum.

When, in 1917, the last surviving member of the family, Victor Depaz, returned to rebuild the shattered business he discovered the unlooked-for bounty of volcanic ash that was to be the key to this rum's exceptional flavour (probably best not to contemplate the likely contents of said ash). Today, the Depaz distillery is considered by many connoisseurs to be one of Martinique's finest. The company, like Negrita, J. Bally and Dillon, is part of the French group La Martiniquaise, and so its products are most easily found in France.

Rhum agricole is a distinct category, and production of the best rhum in Martinique is subject to strict Appellation d'Origine Contrôlée regulations. The style is very different to the sweet and sweetened taste that characterises more industrial rum, but agricole represents a mere 3% or less of world production and is a truly artisanal process, dictated by harvests in much the same way as wine.

It can be robust and vegetal, but here, using the highest quality of cane that is grown on the Chateau Depaz Estate and processed immediately after harvesting, it approaches a level of complexity that stands comparison with any great spirit. Once aged, it could be mistaken for a good cognac.

The Blanc, or Cuvée de la Montagne, sampled here is the nearest thing to 'new make' that Depaz offer and, despite a 45% ABV bottling strength, quite agreeable taken neat. Unfortunately, however, production is necessarily limited and, with the brand popular in France, hard to find in the UK.

Do not let that deter you. Take a quick trip across *La Manche* and track down a bottle or three. The estate was first planted in 1651 so has been waiting for you for some while. Seek it out!

35

DEPAZ XO

Brand owner: La Martiniquaise
Website: www.depazrhum.com
Origin: Martinique

I'M SORRY TO GO ON ABOUT THESE RUMS FROM DEPAZ, AS THEY are so very hard to find in the UK. Actually, I'm only a bit sorry as, having discovered their remarkable quality and value, I'm more than happy to share that knowledge in the hope that the brand owner (ultimately the giant La Martiniquaise) will find a competent distributor here. I don't see why the French should keep them all to themselves, though I can quite see why they might want to.

However, you can find them online without too much trouble, and an agreeable alternative might be a quick dash to one of the huge booze warehouses that surround many of the Channel ports where the competitive prices compensate for the less than glamorous setting.

Depaz's extensive range follows the cognac style of designation, rather than using more straightforward age statements, and runs from a white rum (Blanc) to the super-premium Cuvée Prestige. On second thought, make that merely 'premium', as I can find it available at under €90, which is cracking value.

But this XO – Hors d'Âge, to use the appropriate terminology – is to be found for the more modest sum of €60 or so and I simply can't ignore the bargain that this represents. The blend uses rum of eight to ten years of age and, bearing in mind that rum ages faster than Scotch due to the climate in which it matures, is super-smooth, rich and surprisingly sweet (not cloyingly so, merely agreeably warming and mouth-coating). It is dangerously more-ish.

The VSOP (Very Superior Old Pale), as brandy drinkers will appreciate, is slightly younger (around seven years) and consequently a little cheaper. It's somewhat reminiscent of brandy, curiously enough, and rather hotter than its older sibling, the XO, which is assuredly a rum of power and distinction. It's certainly enjoyable, but for my money I'd take the older version every time.

These really do show us how the rhum agricole style can be one of great distinction and flair, capable of standing against any other fine spirit. 'Agricole' translates literally into English as 'agricultural', not always a term of praise. But much has been lost in translation here and it would be a grave mistake to consider these as anything other than sophisticated products that would satisfy the most discerning of palates. Such as yours, dear reader.

36

DILLON VSOP

Brand owner: La Martiniquaise
Website: www.rhums-dillon.com
Origin: Martinique

WIDELY AVAILABLE IN FRANCE, DILLON (ANOTHER MEMBER OF THE LA Martiniquaise group) offer a range of rhums agricole from their distillery in Fort-de-France, the capital of Martinique. The estate on which it is based was first settled in 1690 but is today named after an English soldier, Arthur Dillon. In an eventful life, he fought with the French troops in the Caribbean on the side of the colonists in the American War of Independence, hence the 1779 date embossed on the bottle.

Following the death of his first wife, he married a wealthy French Creole widow from Martinique, Laure, Comtesse de la Touche and acquired the estate that carries his name. Unluckily for him, he later served as a Deputy in the revolutionary government in Paris but fell under suspicion during the Reign of Terror and was guillotined in April 1794. Curiously enough, the brand's website omits any reference to his unfortunate end.

But back to the rum, which in accordance with the AOC rules is 100% sugar cane, of which some ten varieties in all are used. Once harvesting of the two-year-old cane begins, speed is of the essence – 'the cane should have its feet in the earth and its head in the mill', say the distillers – and all the sugar is extracted in just two to three days, using a steam-powered mill fired by the dried spent cane, or *bagasse*. It's rather satisfying to encounter such well-established sustainable working methods in this era of environmental responsibility.

Since 1996, the strict AOC rules help guarantee the quality of rhum agricole from Martinique, limiting yields, fixing harvesting dates, specifying the exclusive use of cane sugar and setting minimum ageing times.

This VSOP expression has been aged for a minimum of five years and shows chocolate, dried fruits, cinnamon, liquorice and delicate vanilla aromas. The finish is bizarrely reminiscent of pastis, but this is a product which, like the younger expressions, works very well in various rum cocktails and even in cooking.

Though little seen in the UK, it's found very easily in France where it is competitively priced. The older expressions work well as sipping rums or for serving with a sweet dessert tart.

37

DIPLOMÁTICO RESERVA EXCLUSIVA

Brand owner: Destilerías Unidas S. A.
Website: www.rondiplomatico.com
Origin: Venezuela

THE CRUSTY OLD BOY ON THE LABEL, IN CASE YOU WERE WONDERING, is one Don Juancho Nieto Meléndez, a fellow of refined taste and sensibility. Apparently, he used to live near the distillery – except it wasn't built then so he's not really got very much to do with this rum at all. Perhaps the designer liked his stylish face fungus.

I got rather lost in all this and, before I sampled the rum itself, grew the tiniest bit cynical about the plethora of awards garnered by this distillery and their Maestros Roneros, Tito Cordero, Gilberto Briceño and Nelson Hernández. Surely it couldn't possibly be as good as suggested, especially for £40. And if these guys are so special, why not make them the heroes instead of Señor Meléndez?

But I was wrong! It's not just PR hype and spin. It's actually better than the plaudits would have you believe. This is a distilled spirit of truly exceptional quality, especially when you consider that it's aged for up to 12 years. All the good things you'll hear about this are true.

The distillery itself was only founded in 1959, remains in local ownership and is one of the largest distilling groups in Venezuela. Over the years, a complex distillation, maturation and blending regime has been developed that, taken as a whole, is probably unique.

Elements of their approach may be seen elsewhere but this particular combination of art and science is quite distinctive. If you're interested in the technical aspects, take a look at their excellent and very clear website; otherwise, just believe me (and lots of highly experienced judges) that everything you really need to know becomes apparent from the first sip.

Right from *my* first sip, I really was entranced by its power, majesty and balance; this is a rich, fruity and complex spirit. I should in all fairness add the caveat that it is quite sweet – not cloyingly so and not out of balance, but definitely on the sweet end of the spectrum. Diplomático is one of those rums that add sugar to the final blend, a practice that deeply offends some purists. If you like a drier style you probably won't care for this but approach it with an open mind and be prepared for a treat.

38

DON Q GRAN AÑEJO

Brand owner: Destilería Serrallés, Inc.
Website: www.donq.com
Origin: Puerto Rico

PUERTO RICO IS PROBABLY BEST KNOWN FOR BEING THE HOME OF Bacardí and their giant distillery, which is located just outside the capital, San Juan. But they are far from the only distiller on the island, and a principal local rival with a growing international reputation is the Destilería Serrallés, based in Ponce. Like Bacardí, it remains privately owned, with the sixth generation of the Serrallés family in charge today. It's a curious bit of rum trivia to note that the spirit for the Captain Morgan brand was also made here for many years, but production switched to a Diageo-owned facility in the US Virgin Islands in 2012.

The Don Q brand was launched at the distillery's foundation in 1865 and, as you've probably guessed, is named after Don Quixote, the titular character from Cervantes' novel, in a nod to the family's Spanish origins.

There are a number of different expressions under the Don Q label but, leaving out the £1,500 Reserva de la Familia Serrallés, they are mostly relatively modestly priced. Even this top of the range Gran Añejo, a blend of Puerto Rican rums between nine and 12 years (with some solera aged rums up to 50 years), is only £50 or so. For that money you could do a great deal worse.

Though initially quite subtle on the nose, it's quite an assertive drop, with notable rich molasses and wood notes, but tempered by dark vine fruits and vanilla, creating an intriguing balance between sweet and dry flavours. Behind this lies the distilling regime: Serrallés maintain both pot and column stills and both are used in the final blend, which is aged in American oak and former sherry casks, with a marrying vat to aid the merging of the different strains.

Environmental considerations, such as energy usage and waste water disposal, are of growing importance to the distilling industry. As a locally owned producer, the Serrallés family seem particularly conscious of this and have pioneered cutting-edge waste reclamation processes to make theirs a notably green distillery. At a cultural level, the original family home, Castillo Serrallés, was passed to the City of Ponce in 2001 for a nominal fee, and now operates as a museum and cultural venue. I had the privilege of visiting this some years ago, and the taste of this Gran Añejo brings back happy memories.

39

DOORLY'S 12 YEAR OLD

Brand owner: R. L. Seale & Co Ltd
Website: none
Origin: Barbados

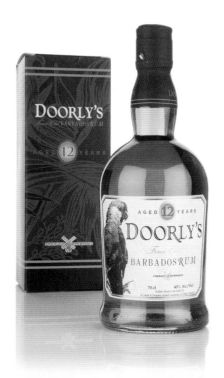

THERE ARE QUITE A NUMBER OF AGED RUMS ON OFFER IN THE Doorly's range, which is produced at the famous Foursquare distillery in Barbados by the R. L. Seale company. I thought I'd go to the top of the range, as they're not expensive and their reputation goes before them. But given that they offer other expressions under the Foursquare and Seale brand names, you might ask what exactly is going on. And who is Doorly?

Well, originally Doorly's were a trading company who, around a century ago, got into bottling at a time when the distillers themselves were obliged by law to sell in bulk. They created Doorly's Macaw Rum, which became the first bottled rum to be exported from Barbados. The brand rights were then acquired by the Foursquare distillery in 1993 and they developed and extended the range.

This 12-year-old version is actually quite a recent – and eagerly awaited – arrival on UK shores, having been launched in 2015. Prior to that it was reputedly available only at the distillery and at a few privileged outlets in Barbados. It stands apart from the other rums from Foursquare due to the current head distiller Richard Seale's innovative approach to distilling and blending.

All those skills are showcased here. Seale has taken his pot and column still rums and blended casks aged for 12 years in ex-bourbon barrels (90%) with the remainder drawn from Madeira casks for sweetness, again aged for 12 years in wood. The rums are then married for a short period to allow the flavours to fully integrate, then bottled at 40%.

Foursquare are notable for offering very fair value and being completely transparent in describing their products. Despite its relative advanced age, the 12 Year Old isn't presented in a lavish box, but is content with a simple carton and relatively plain bottle, with a screw cap, all of which keeps the cost down for you, the consumer.

Incidentally, the pretty boy on the label isn't, as you might imagine, a parrot but a macaw (didn't you read the second paragraph?). And not just any macaw, but the desperately rare Spix's Macaw, now thought to be extinct in the wild. Fortunately, while Doorly's 12 Year Old is hard to find, some bottles can be found in captivity, in independent off-licences.

40

DOS MADERAS 5 + 5 PX

Brand owner: Bodegas Williams & Humbert
Website: www.rondosmaderas.com
Origin: Blend

'IF MACALLAN MADE RUM AND PRODUCED THIS BOTTLE, IT WOULD
BE £200!'

Not my opinion but a consumer review, presumably genuine, from
the Master of Malt website. The Dos Maderas 5 + 5 is actually priced
at around £40, but I think the reviewer may have put their finger on
rum's incredible value. This is why so many previously enthusiastic
whisky drinkers are turning to rum, where they see the combination
of intriguing backstory, product and heritage that first attracted them
to Scotch without the ritzy packaging and ever higher prices.

Dos Maderas is the Spanish for 'two woods' and describes the process
of Caribbean and sherry cask ageing that are at the heart of the
flavour profiles here. Five-year-old rums from Guyana and Barbados
are chosen and, once shipped to the Williams & Humbert bodegas
in Jerez de la Frontera in Spain, refilled without filtration into
American oak casks, some more than 80 years old. This exceptionally
dense wood has long been used for the ageing of very old sherry and
Williams & Humbert have many years experience in managing their
solera process.

Once in Spain, the rum spends three years in casks previously used to
age a rare, award-winning Palo Cortado. This sherry is dry, but very
aromatic. This is Dos Maderas 5 + 3 rum, denoting five years in the
Caribbean and three in Jerez. That's unusual enough in itself.

But onwards! The rum not bottled as 5 + 3 is then added for a further
two years to casks which have previously been used to age 20-year-
old Pedro Ximénez sherry. Pedro Ximénez is an intensely sweet, but
not cloying, dark sherry made from grapes that, once harvested, are
left out in the Andalusian sunshine to become raisins.

This period of ageing in 'PX' casks transforms the rum, giving it a
darker colour and its very distinctive smooth and sweet flavour. This
is Dos Maderas 5 + 5 PX: five years in the Caribbean, plus three years
in Palo Cortado casks and two in Pedro Ximénez.

If your budget runs to it, for around £120 there is the even more
remarkable Dos Maderas Luxus 10 + 5 version, comprising ten-year-
old Guyanese and Barbadian rums, aged in the Pedro Ximénez casks
for a further five years. Try not to think what the equivalent single
malt would cost.

41

EL DORADO 15 YEAR OLD SPECIAL RESERVE

Brand owner: Demerara Distillers Ltd
Website: www.theeldoradorum.com
Origin: Guyana

DEMERARA DISTILLERS ARE BASED IN GUYANA, HOME TO THE original El Dorado, the 'City of Gold'; a mythical place that so entranced early European explorers that many died in the attempt to find it. Clearly, they wanted a name with local resonance and one which conveyed the remarkable quality of this product. Well, they chose well: quite simply, this is one of the world's great rums, one of the most awarded and one of the most influential.

Today, the distillery is renowned for having a collection of stills that are legendary in rum-drinking circles: one of the very last surviving wooden Coffey stills to be found anywhere in the world; a double wooden pot still from Port Mourant; a single wooden pot still and a four-column metal French Savalle still inherited from the eighteenth-century Uitvlugt Estate. These pieces of equipment represent a distilling time machine and are spoken of in hushed terms. Vintage rums known to be distilled on the Port Mourant or Uitvlugt stills fetch very high prices at auction today, as connoisseurs vie for a taste of history.

But for around £50 you can have a slice of that history with this remarkable 15 Year Old Special Reserve. Better judges than me (the IWSC panel, to be precise) rated this 'Best Rum in the World' four years running and that is an extraordinary achievement. It was also one of the first rums to show the world that premium quality was possible in what had been, until this was launched, something of an undervalued and underappreciated category.

That's arguably still true today, though less so. An example of rum hiding its light under a bushel, however, is the distillery's own website that describes this as 'a fine, cognac-like rum'. I don't see the need for the cognac comparison, as if genuflecting to some superior being. Rum today has nothing to apologise for when there are products like this to enjoy.

For me, this Special Reserve represents exceptional value for money. This is rich, enveloping and deep; packed with dark coffee, bitter orange marmalade, almonds, 70% chocolate, prunes and rich vanilla. It's sweet but never excessively so – I'd love to try this before dilution for bottling. The City of Gold may have been myth, but it would have been a happy conquistador who returned home in triumph with this wonderful booty.

42

ELEMENTS EIGHT
REPUBLICA

Brand owner: Elements Eight Rum Company Ltd
Website: www.e8rum.com
Origin: Blend

IF YOU STUDIED CHEMISTRY (WHICH I DIDN'T, SO I LOOKED IT UP), you'll know there are 118 elements in the Periodic Table. These guys manage with just eight. So what are they?

Glad you asked. Referring to the stylish label, they are (in this order), Terroir, Cane, Water, Fermentation, Distillation, Tropical Aging, Blending and Filtration. Which is curious, because this list conflates ingredients with processes, and as this comes in a bottle that really makes nine (Bottling?). What's more, if you think about it, these elements are shared by pretty well everyone who makes rum. And while the label clearly tells us that this has been 'distilled in traditional column stills', the symbol for Distillation is quite obviously a pot still.

Enough pedantry! Elements Eight is a British independent bottler, established in 2006, which has enjoyed some success as a 'bartender's brand', by which we can take it that it was launched initially in pubs and clubs. That's a well-enough recognised strategy by which many drinks brands have been developed. Given that they now have four rums in their range, and Elements can be found in better off-licences, it's evidently working well for them.

Republica is a blend of two five-year-old rums from Cuba and Panama (both republics, you see) and a very pleasant drop it is too. According to the company's website, their rums are 'a labour of love and with passion comes unexpected results. Our rums are smoother and more complex than conventional rum brands.'

I'm not sure if I'd go that far, but all credit to Elements' Carl Stephenson, who created this. He's an advocate of 'unadulterated' rums, which can be tricky to find in Cuba and Panama. However, he has worked with Varela Hermanos in Panama and Distilleria Cubay in Cuba to source 100% multi-column distilled, non-chill filtered distillates, which are aged for a minimum of five years in their respective countries. Independent tests confirm the absence of sugar so, if this matters to you, you can go ahead and enjoy.

It reminded me a little of a fruit cake, generously laden with raisins and prunes and with a tantalising hint of a gentle, sweet ginger. It works well in classic cocktails (hence the emphasis on bar serves) and, at around £30, represents decent value for money.

43

FACUNDO NEO

Brand owner: Bacardi and Company Ltd
Website: www.facundorum.com
Origin: Puerto Rico

WHAT ARE YOU TO DO WHEN YOU'VE BUILT A REPUTATION AND A solid business on the mass market and the consumer starts to move upmarket? It's a tricky marketing problem, and an especially sensitive one when, like Bacardí, the company remains in family ownership and the family name is on every bottle.

Bacardí's answer was to raid the family's private reserves in order to launch a line of products based on their heritage but with a very distinctly different positioning and with a taste strikingly different to the regular product line. They called this new range Facundo, after the company's founder, Don Facundo Bacardí Massó, and then draped the packaging with references to the company's history.

The admittedly rather dapper bottle for the entry-level Neo expression (a relative term, incidentally, as this is two to three times the price of Bacardí's Carta Blanca) features Bacardí's original offices in Santiago de Cuba and is, according to the Facundo website, 'an ode' to this architectural legacy.

By the time we reach the ultimate Paraíso (£255) the bottle design is 'steeped in Cuban tradition and the heritage of Bacardí', using details from their original Santiago distillery and the magificent Edificio Bacardí in Havana (which, to be fair, is a world-class example of Art Deco). There is also a large bat logo front and centre, just in case anyone was in any doubt who made the rum.

This, of course, assumes that you know and – perhaps an even greater leap – actually care about the various Bacardí properties, most of which aren't theirs anymore. I can see that this matters to the family who to this day burn with the injustice of their exile from Cuba, but I'm not sure that consumers are greatly concerned when deciding on an expensive after-dinner digestif. However, in a highly competitive market, Bacardí are understandably anxious to take every opportunity to remind us of their roots and so we are treated to this Pevsner-style architectural grand tour in glass.

Neo is an unusual silver rum (posh name for white, methinks) that, somewhat eccentrically, has been aged up to eight years, blended and then charcoal filtered to remove the colour. It didn't seem all that rum-like, to my admittedly unsubtle palate. All three of the more expensive big brothers in the range – Eximo, Exquisito and Paraíso – carry extra age and are dark in colour.

44

FLOR DE CAÑA 12 YEAR

Brand owner: Compañía Licorera de Nicaragua, S. A.
Website: www.flordecana.com
Origin: Nicaragua

WHILE LESSER RUMS HAVE STANDARD OR ENTRY-LEVEL EXPRESSIONS, the Flor de Caña website boldly offers only 'Premium', 'Super Premium' and 'Ultra Premium' collections. No false modesty here, then.

In fairness, as they go on to remind us, Flor de Caña have 'received over 180 international accolades and have won five times the recognition as the Best Rum in the World at competitions in London, Chicago and San Francisco. Flor de Caña is the leading brand in Central America and Nicaragua's #1 exported brand.'

So, faced with that, I thought we should skip the mere Premium and Super Premium rums and go straight to the entry-level (oops, sorry, misspoke there) Ultra Premium 12 Year. Note in passing that there are two more in the collection at 18 and 25 years of age and they're not bad value. For example, the 25-year-old is currently under £125. Compare this to a similarly aged single malt Scotch, while bearing in mind that the rum will have aged faster and lost more to the angels, and the value here is immediately apparent.

Hold that thought. At 12 years of age, this shows great maturity. Whether that is anything to do with the nearby San Cristobal volcano which, rather fancifully, I feel, lets the website claim this is a 'volcano-enriched spirit', I don't know. Despite the fact that San Cristobal volcano is active, the family behind the business have been there for over 125 years and should at least be commended for their remarkably stoic attitude.

Such patience also contributed to the significant quantities of aged rum that are now available to them. In the 1980s, domestic consumption fell during a period of political instability and very high inflation, but being a well-founded family business, the distillery continued in production and the rum consequently enjoyed unusually lengthy maturation. Today, the company benefits from this legacy and rum drinkers are able to enjoy great aged rums at reasonable cost.

This 12-year-old is super stuff. It's also good to know that the distillery is entirely powered by renewable energy, that they plant 50,000 trees annually to protect their water sources and recycle tons of cardboard and glass, all of which has prompted their many environmental awards. Let's just hope that San Cristobal continues to behave: it would be a shame to bury all this under hot lava.

45

FOURSQUARE CASK STRENGTH (2004)

Brand owner: R. L. Seale & Co Ltd
Website: None
Origin: Barbados

ONE OF THE GREAT PROBLEMS THAT CONFRONTS RUM AS A CATEGORY – at least in the opinion of many people who make and sell it – is that there is no agreed basis for classification. That's because rum is made in so many different places that no one can agree on a common basis for the rules. What is permitted in one country is banned elsewhere and that can lead to confusion as to what labels actually mean.

Major award schemes attempt to discriminate by colour (White, Golden, Dark and Flavoured, for example) but that just leads to more confusion as rums of the 'same' colour may, in fact, be fundamentally different. To make things worse, not every rum producer is completely enthusiastic about full transparency either, and that adds another dimension to the problem.

Having said all that, I'm not completely convinced that many consumers care all that much – though arguably they jolly well should. And anyway, one can hardly have too much information. So, kudos to Richard Seale of Foursquare who has adopted the classification system proposed by Luca Gargano of the Habitation Velier rum project.

That's why you can read on this label the words 'Single Blended Rum'. That indicates that what we have here is a blend of only pot still and traditional column still rums, in this case from the R. L. Seale distillery in Barbados. A 'traditional' column still is distinct from the multi-column plants that produce light rum in a 'modern' style. As Seale rightly says, 'by all means drink what you enjoy, but at least know what you are drinking'.

It's been bottled at full cask strength (a mighty 59%) after 11 years maturation in American oak ex-bourbon casks and is part of the distillery's Exceptional Cask series: a range of limited edition bottlings released in relatively small quantities. You probably won't drink this at full strength (well, you can if you want) but the point of the cask strength is that you can experiment with dilution until you find exactly the right proportion of rum and mixer for your palate. Which is fun.

Expect Seale's trademark style, notably drier and spicier than the sweetened rums of his competitors. Lots of depth of flavour; notes of golden syrup, dried fruits, dark chocolate and drying spices on the finish. Yum!

46

FOURSQUARE SPICED

Brand owner: R. L. Seale & Co Ltd
Website: None
Origin: Barbados

IGNORE THE 'SPICE' WORD FOR THE MOMENT, BECAUSE YOU'RE IN good hands. This is a product of the esteemed Richard Seale (rum aristocracy) and his Foursquare Distillery in Barbados. It may be housed in an old sugar factory that dates back to 1636 but today is home to one of the most modern and efficient rum distilleries in the world.

For me anyway, spiced rum is all about balance. Some are cloyingly sweet and some overdo the spices, particularly the vanilla, but I maintain that this hits the spot. Purists decry the trend to spiced rum – and for the greater part, I take their point – but this feels just right. There's a cinnamon note quite evident, and cloves and nutmeg and ginger too, but behind it you'll never forget that you're getting a decent rum base. Actually, and very agreeably, it reminds me of the spiced German buns that you sometimes get at Christmas and perhaps, a little bit, of the old-fashioned hot cross buns of my dimly remembered childhood. This is a good thing.

You could happily drink this neat, over ice and with a decent ginger ale, or, for stunning results, you could use it to make a delicious spicy Mojito. I'd assume from the relatively modest price point (sub £25) that the rums here are fairly young, but even so there's no rawness or alcohol burn, though that may be down to the relatively modest 37.5% alcohol content (which in turn helps the price, so round we go).

Importantly, it hasn't been artificially sweetened with added sugar. Seale is something of a zealot on the question of sugar dosing, but that means there is no cloak of sweetness for his products to hide inside. This is said to be a secret family recipe passed down through five generations, in which case it predates the current fashion for spiced rums.

It's a shame, then, that some of the more recent interlopers didn't take a lesson from this, because if they had then spiced rum wouldn't have the rather dubious reputation that clings to it today, amongst serious rum afficionados at least.

If that's you, I'd urge you to approach this with an open mind and give it a fair try. On the other hand, if you simply like nice, tasty things and don't want to spend a king's ransom on your drinks, you may snap this up with confidence.

47

GOSLING'S BLACK SEAL 151

Brand owner: Gosling Brothers Ltd
Website: www.goslingsrum.com
Origin: Bermuda

NOW PAY ATTENTION. IT'S NOT CALLED 151 FOR NOTHING. 151 indicates the proof strength of this Bermudian blaster – that's 75.5% ABV in real money – so this is to be handled with care.

It comes in a no-nonsense tall round bottle and, because it's called Black Seal, there's a picture of a black seal on the label, juggling a barrel of rum on his nose, as all good seals should do. Apparently, though, it was named not for the versatile marine mammal that graces the packaging but because the earliest bottlings of Gosling's rum were in old champagne bottles closed with, you've guessed, black sealing wax.

And where did they get old champagne bottles, you may reasonably ask. Apparently, in an early example of inspired recycling, they came from the British officers' mess.

The family, who still own and run the business, have been based in Bermuda since 1806, and first started blending rums around 1860. Today all their rums, but especially their Black Seal, are recognised as rum classics. This bad boy is available at the standard 40% ABV strength and, occasionally, at 70% (140 proof) but if you're going that far, why stop there? So 151 it is.

Of course, though it's remarkably smoooth for the strength, you won't be drinking this neat (if you are doing so regularly, get help). It serves very well in a cocktail, because the rum punches through all sorts of different mixers, delivering a mighty blast of intense liquorice, molasses and spice.

However, the classic serve is the Dark 'N' Stormy, created on Bermuda around the time of World War I, for which Gosling's own the USA copyright, so do the right thing and only ever make yours with their rum.

The officially recommended partner here is Barritt's Ginger Beer, but as you aren't going to be able to find that, do as I did and mix with Fever-Tree's Smoky Ginger Ale. That really works well.

At first glance, a bottle may look expensive, at just under £40, but don't forget the remarkable strength. At 75.5% it's the equivalent of two of those high street standards that have been bottled at a puny 37.5%. Quite simply, you get what you pay for.

48

HAVANA CLUB 7 YEARS

Brand owner: Havana Club Holding S. A. / Pernod Ricard
Website: www.havana-club.com
Origin: Cuba

MUCH THOUGH I WOULD LIKE TO INCLUDE ALL THE RUMS FROM Havana Club – yes, they are that good – I don't have space. And there simply aren't enough pages to explain the long-running and intensely fought legal dispute between Bacardí and Pernod Ricard over the use of the Havana Club brand name: that would require a whole book unto itself. Suffice it for you to be aware that if you buy 'Havana Club' in the US it has in all probability been distilled by Bacardí in Puerto Rico (which is both completely legal there and perfectly lovely, lawyers please note), while elsewhere in the world, your bottle of Havana Club has almost certainly been distilled in Cuba and distributed and marketed by Pernod Ricard, who have a joint venture with the Cuban government.

Incidentally, it looks as if the litigation will continue until one side runs out of money which, given the size and wealth of the protagonists, is very good news indeed for the lawyers. Aren't we all perfectly delighted for them?

But moving on and limiting myself to just two Havana Clubs (both from the Cuban side), this very soon became a firm favourite in my drinking repertoire. Thing is, the standard Añejo Especial and the three-year-old white rum are really very good, but this is just better – and you pick that up as soon as you compare it with its younger relatives. You can mix this or drink it neat; either way, it performs, and for the slight premium in price it's well worth paying extra.

Seven years old is actually quite a modest claim. Havana Club refer to the art of *añejamiento*, or distilling, ageing and blending, and this expression is made up of a complex blend of different rum bases that undergo a further process of continuous ageing, pioneered in the late 1960s by the Maestros del Ron Cubano. A small proportion of each blend is always reserved for the next batch, thus ensuring that every bottle retains a trace of the very first blend. That may sound a little like a homeopathic approach to blending, but the proof is in the bottle and that's good enough for me.

Incidentally, to qualify as a Maestro Ronero requires an apprenticeship of 15 years, so be assured that these folks are deeply committed to their craft.

For the avoidance of doubt, Havana Club in the USA is a completely different product.

49

HAVANA CLUB MÁXIMO EXTRA AÑEJO

Brand owner: Havana Club Holding S. A. / Pernod Ricard
Website: www.havana-club.com
Origin: Cuba

EXERCISING MY WELL-KNOWN RESTRAINT, I DECIDED TO LIMIT myself to just two rums from the Havana Club range. That was a tough call, believe me, and required some self-discipline. But while the seven-year-old really chose itself, I pondered my second selection at some length.

I'm not usually a fan of things with four-figure price tags, but I thought I could squeeze just one ultra-premium bottle in here. You might, after all, be a hedge fund manager – or a dentist – so something quite extravagant was clearly called for. Believe it or not, there are a few £1,000+ rums to chose from. Though rum is yet to get quite as silly as single malt whiskies, it's clearly trying its best.

This will cost you around £1,250 for just 50 cl. That's more than £1,700 for the equivalent of a standard bottle. Or, to put it another way, about £62.50 for a single pub measure.

Clearly, if you can afford £1,250, the price isn't the issue. Getting your hands on a bottle might be, though, as they only release 1,000 bottles annually. Whether that's because that makes it more desirable or because they only have stock enough for 1,000 I have no idea, but there you are. Get one while you can.

It's very, very good, but products like this exist in a somewhat rarefied world of their own and comparisons with lesser rums aren't really the point.

Máximo Extra Añejo is drawn from the oldest and rarest of Cuban rums, blended by Havana Club's Maestro Ronero, Don José Navarro, and then beautifully packaged in a handmade crystal decanter with a crystal stopper carrying an etching of Havana's iconic Giraldilla (you won't be taking this to the recycling bin).

I'm happy to tell you that it's an extraordinarily rich, complex and subtle product. It won't change your life, but it will make you feel a great deal better about it for some while after you drain the glass. It's one to take very slowly, not because of the price (well, yes, a little bit because of the price) but because of its remarkable evolution. As it breathes in the glass, so it changes and develops, showing layers of captivating aromas and flavours. Trust me, as you probably must: drinking this is a unique and special privilege that has to be savoured.

50

J. GOW SPICED

Brand owner: VS Distillers Ltd
Website: www.jgowrum.com
Origin: Scotland

Essential requirement for new rum brand # 1: distillery on a remote and exotic island – Check

Essential requirement for new rum brand # 2: Pirate story – Check

Essential requirement for new rum brand # 3: Locally sourced ingredients – Check

Essential requirement for new rum brand # 4: Hot and humid climate – Er, no . . .

WHAT ON EARTH'S GOING ON HERE? WELL, VS DISTILLERS (VERY NEW, but distillers all the same) are on an island, and they do have their own pirate story and some local ingredients, but the island is Lamb Holm, part of the Orkney islands, and the pirate is local bad boy John Gow. He came to a sticky end on London's Execution Dock, where the Admiralty hung pirates in a particularly gruesome manner, and was 'turned off' – not very 'woke', I know, but it's the correct eighteenth-century term – on 11 June 1725 (which was a Monday, as it happens).

In fact, so notorious was Gow that they hanged him twice, just to make sure, then tarred his body and left it hanging in the Thames until three tides had washed over it. Anyway, he became quite famous. Daniel Defoe wrote an account of his short and violent life (Gow wasn't a terribly nice fellow, truth to tell) and Gilbert and Sullivan freely adapted his story for their light operetta *The Pirates of Penzance*. Now he has a rum named in his honour, though that doesn't seem quite the correct term for this nasty piece of work.

Orkney is quite the place for distilling these days. Great single malt whisky is made there and some decent gin as well. VS Distillers is a new venture by Collin van Schayk of the family-run Orkney Wine Company. 'We were looking at how we could diversify the business and do something different that wasn't gin or whisky,' he told me. 'We all like rum, so it was an obvious choice. It's a first for Orkney and fits in well with the seafaring traditions of the islands.'

Casks are being laid down for a pure rum but, in the meantime, they've released this spiced version. It's not half bad. Quite gingery and with lots of cinnamon, but unsweetened, and bottled at the proper 40% strength.

And the 'local ingredients'? Well, they're secret, of course. That's an essential requirement.

51

J. WRAY & NEPHEW WHITE OVERPROOF

Brand owner: Gruppo Campari
Website: www.straightfromyard.co.uk
Origin: Jamaica

OVERPROOF IS VERY DEFINITELY A THING IN JAMAICA, AND WRAY &
Nephew's Overproof is *the* thing. Thing is, it means what it says:
Overproof. It's bottled at a mighty 63%, so you might want to take
it carefully at first. And probably for quite a while after that.

Today, Wray & Nephew is part of the Italian Gruppo Campari (they
also control the Appleton brand). First established in 1825, today it's a
big business, with an estate growing more than 11,000 acres of sugar
cane, a sugar cane refinery, and the distillery itself.

I'd suggest it was the dinosaur of rum, but that would be wrong.
The dinosaurs are all gone and yet Overproof lives. So, Overproof
feels like something of a coelacanth – a survivor from another
time that's doing just fine, thank you very much. Best for the
marketing boys and girls to leave well alone: the simple packaging
and uncompromising product know just what they're about and,
as it's said that 90% of all the rum sold in Jamaica is from Wray &
Nephew, something is clearly being done right.

You won't, of course, be drinking this neat (or at least you shouldn't
be). How this works best is in mixed drinks, where the fruity natural
aroma with overtones of molasses works wonderfully well. But this is
not just a massively strong hit of crude alcohol. There is complexity
here, which adds weight to cocktails, and perhaps surprisingly it
doesn't really bite. This, of course, makes it all the more dangerous to
the uniniated or unaware!

Its complexity adds a unique character to cocktails and is the
essential ingredient in an authentically full-flavoured Jamaican rum
punch (there's so much fruit in some versions of these that a glassful
could be one of your five a day, though strictly speaking this may not
be medically recommended).

But what you have here is a cultural icon, as much a part of Jamaica
as whisky is to Scotland. As such, it is a local legend that has
transcended mere alcohol – a very potent spirit indeed.

It's relatively easy to find on the high street at under £25, and
so constitutes a remarkable bargain as long as you look past the
utilitarian packaging, understand what you've bought and – as the
drinks industry likes to remind us – use the product responsibly.
It's up to you!

52

JEFFERSON'S EXTRA FINE

Brand owner: Whitehaven Harbour Commissioners
Website: www.rumstory.co.uk
Origin: Blend

TAKE YOURSELF OFF TO WHITEHAVEN, A SMALL CUMBRIAN COASTAL town north of the Lake District. It has a fascinating history, a largely intact historic Georgian townplan, some lovely domestic Georgian architecture (though, sadly, many of the houses appear in need of extensive and immediate restoration) and an exhibition centre dedicated to the history of rum. It's the only one of its kind in the UK and well worth a visit.

The ingeniously named Rum Story tells the story of – well, you've probably worked out what you'll find there. Whitehaven was a successful and prosperous port in the eighteenth century (and the target of a celebrated attack by the American Navy in April 1778). Since then, it has suffered a long economic decline.

Jefferson's, a family firm of wine and spirit merchants, was founded in 1734, and from 1785 they engaged in the production of rum on the family estates in Antigua. Theirs was said to be the oldest label in the United Kingdom. Once a flourishing business with interests well beyond the spirits trade, Jefferson's closed in June 1998 and their premises, much of which had remained untouched for many decades, were converted to The Rum Story in an attempt to draw visitors to the town.

Among the many points of interest there is a wonderful short film on the production of rum in the splendidly antiquated pot stills of Rivers rum on the River Antoine Estate in Grenada (frustratingly, all but unobtainable outside of Grenada).

However, once you've absorbed all the displays and read the many text panels, you will feel the urge to visit the small shop and buy some rum. And, what do you know, they've thought of that! Bottles of Jefferson's Extra Fine Dark Rum are available for a perfectly reasonable £30. It's an excellent Navy-style dark rum, which my spies tell me is most probably a blend of pot and column distilled rums from Guyana and Jamaica. Or if you feel like splashing out, there is the 24-year-old limited edition expression for around £100.

Whatever the exact make-up of the final blend, it's a worthy tribute to and legacy of the lost Jefferson empire. There is an attractive burnt-sugar nose, tons of spice and more than a hint of treacle, which means this stands up to ice and comes through well when mixed or in a cocktail.

53

THE KRAKEN
BLACK SPICED RUM

Brand owner: Proximo Spirits
Website: www.krakenrum.com
Origin: Trinidad

YOU WOULDN'T WANT TO MEET A REAL-LIFE KRAKEN AND YOU certainly wouldn't want to mess with one. Fortunately, this is a creature of myth and legend, thought to have been based on early seafarers' sightings of giant squid or colossal octopuses[4], but pioneering mariners and naturalists did once believe in the mythical beast, and very scary it must have seemed.

Today, drinks industry marketing folk regard The Kraken with the same sense of fear and stunned respect as did ancient seadogs. They gaze in horrified shock and awe at The Kraken Black Spiced Rum's astonishing growth which, since its 2010 launch in the USA (it took the behemoth around a year to cross the Atlantic, no doubt terrifying a few sailors on the way), has been nothing short of a marketing phenomenon. It is one of the fastest-growing rum-based drinks on the market and, so far, its rise has appeared unstoppable.

The product itself is straightforward: a base of Trinidadian rum with a strong molasses influence, aged up to two years and then blended with a mix of 11 spices, including cinnamon, ginger and cloves. It's said to be black, which is how it appears in the bottle, but the liquid itself is more a dark tan. Not that it matters, really, as it will almost certainly be drowned in cola and drunk in the half-light of a nightclub. I thought it was perfectly quaffable, not least because they haven't compromised on strength, though if spiced rum is your thing there are probably more distinctive ones.

What this is mainly about is really good marketing. Starting with the packaging, where a fearsome giant octopus dominates the label, the designers have really understood the steampunk ethos and done an excellent job, especially on the website, which is a joy to behold. The beastie itself could be said to owe something to the illustrative work of the French malacologist[5] Pierre Dénys de Montfort (find him online; you'll see what I mean) but everything about the marketing has been extraordinarily well done. I, for one, wouldn't want to be the brand manager for any of The Kraken's competitors, for fear of being dragged down to Davy Jones's locker.

It's not expensive; huge fun and acceptable at student parties.

---

4   Even though everyone thinks it is, octopi is not actually the correct plural. I expect it's what you were expecting, though.

5   One who studies molluscs. I didn't have to look that up, honest.

54

LOST SPIRITS
NAVY STYLE RUM

Brand owner: Lost Spirits
Website: www.lostspirits.net
Origin: USA

EVER SINCE FOLKS STARTED PUTTING DISTILLED SPIRITS IN barrels and noticing that prolonged storage improved the flavour, accelerating that process has been the holy grail of the industry. It might not be much discussed in public, but over the years there have been many experiments to obtain the benefits of ageing without the lengthy wait or the expense of barrels, warehouses and evaporation.

Scientists, look away now. Grossly simplified, ageing in wood (not necessarily oak, by the way; chestnut has historically been very important) results in important chemical changes to the spirit. New-make distillate is distinguished by short-chain molecules (carboxylic esters and short-chain fatty acids), providing such treats as paint thinner and vinegar in the flavour. However, given time, these short-chain molecules react with the wood to extract tastier new chemicals, notably phenols, benzoic acid, and vanillin, after which a process known as esterification takes place, a source of sweetness, floral elements, hints of nuts and a highly desirable pineapple nose. The off flavours handily disappear along the way. All this takes time, however, and time is money.

Not in the Lost Spirits 'skunk works' in Los Angeles. There, self-taught distiller Bryan Davis has built a 'reactor' that blasts new spirit and pieces of oak with intense light and heat. In as little as six days, the spirit has a chemical signature nearly identical to that of products aged for as long as 20 years and, profiled in a chromatograph, the results are almost indistinguishable. More importantly, it tastes like the real thing.

Navy Style Rum is his flagship product, a cask-strength (68%) tribute to the famous Royal Navy rums of Guyana. Clearly a labour of love, it owes much to the buccaneering influence of disruptive science, Silicon Valley style (this may be the Uber of distilling).

If you didn't know better, you would swear that this had spent many years in the hot and humid Caribbean. The distinctive *rancio* note of aged spirit is there, and though logic tells you that six days in a Star Trek-style 'reactor' cannot possibly deliver the flavours of traditional ageing, your nose and palate tell you otherwise.

Not everyone cares for the potential impact of the Lost Spirits technology but try it blind on a drinks snob and see what happens. Hint: stand well back when you reveal the truth.

55

LOS VALIENTES 20

Brand owner: Licores Veracruz S. A. de C. V.
Website: None
Origin: Mexico

YOU WILL SHORTLY ENCOUNTER THE REMARKABLE SIGHT OF
the Mocambo pistol (at least, you will if reading the book in the
conventional manner; if you started from the back then you'll know
what I'm on about already) and the Los Valientes collection of
aged Mexican rums honours the chaps who carried these pistols
and discharged them in anger. Both come from the same house of
Licores Veracruz.

'Los Valientes' means 'the valiant' and by this the distiller means
the brave and noble soldiers of the local armies who fought in the
Mexican War of Independence (against Spain, as it happens). In
our ignorance and indifference, we probably associate Mexico with
Mayan ruins, violent drug wars or, slightly more positively, tacos
or even Speedy Gonzales ('The Fastest Mouse in all Mexico'). Or
perhaps you share *Top Gear's* childish view of Mexicans, which their
ambassador found 'offensive, xenophobic and humiliating'. However,
I shan't be repeating that here, as Los Valientes has given me such
great and unexpected pleasure.

Whoever would have thought to combine double pot distilled sugar
cane juice (in effect, a rhum agricole) and column still molasses rum,
age it for 20 years, ship it across the Atlantic and still ask less than
£30 for a bottle? OK, it's a half-litre bottle, but it's 43% and still
decent value at the standard bottle equivalent of under £40. Go on,
answer that.

Frankly, I can't, because as far as I can determine this is a one-off. If
this was Scotch whisky, the distiller would charge twice that – at least
– and a disorderly queue would form as customers rushed to grab
some before the distillers came to their senses. This is really quite
delicious: earthy, nutty and a trifle smoky on the nose. There is a note
of truffles on the palate that, quite strangely, reminded me faintly of
old Armagnac, before it faded gently away like a distant mariachi
band. Though Mocambo may be the company's principal rum line,
they have something rather special tucked away here.

The unique formulation, the ageing, the small-batch production in
some very attractive brandy-style alembics and the underlying quality
combine here to create something remarkable that truly justifies the
name Los Valientes. If you had not thought about Mexico for rum –
and I confess that I had not – then you can start and finish here.

56

MARAMA

Brand owner: Beveland Distillers
Website: www.beveland.com
Origin: Fiji

THERE IS SUCH A THING AS A MARAMA RUM PUNCH, BUT THIS ISN'T it, so we need to look deeper at this intriguing offering. It turns out to be a lightly spiced rum from Fiji, of all places, launched only last year in the UK by its Spanish owners, Beveland Distillers, who are also behind Relicario.

This is all part of the richness and fun of rum. Who knew that they made rum in Fiji? Who even suspected that there was a distillery there? I certainly didn't, but one learns something new every day (or at least I did today). 'Marama' means 'lady' in Fijian, which, thanks to the wonders of the world wide web, I have also learned is an Austronesian language of the Malayo-Polynesian family spoken by some 350,000–450,000 ethnic Fijians (a lot more folk than speak Gaelic I realised).

Then again, I could probably have guessed, because the front of the bottle features a mermaid blowing coquettishly on a conch shell whilst riding on the back of a dolphin. This is a reference to the story of a nineteenth-century explorer, one Dr J. Griffin, who is said to have become obsessed with the legend of a Fijian mermaid, claimed to have briefly observed one and then subsequently sank without trace from the pages of history.

However, I fear I am drifting off the point. What you want to know is that this is a column distilled rum using Fijian sugar cane and water that has been filtered through the island's volcanic soil. It is aged three to five years and then exotic plants and native fruits are infused along with spice, vanilla and citrus. Sadly, they rather dominate the base spirit, leaving me with the feeling that I'd like to try Fijian rum in its pure form without the various flavourings.

In truth, it's an undemanding party animal, happy to be served well chilled over cola, to reduce the slightly cloying sweetness that's evident when taken neat.

Marama is a pleasant enough product but, unless I'm very much mistaken, quite possibly as fleeting a visitor to these shores as the elusive mermaid that inspired it. Other, better promoted spiced rums seem likely to take precedence as Marama follows the late and sadly unlamented Dr J. Griffin into myth and legend.

57

MATUGGA GOLDEN RUM

Brand owner: Matugga Beverages
Website: www.matuggarum.com
Origin: England

HERE'S SOMETHING REALLY QUITE UNUSUAL: EAST AFRICAN MOLASSES, distilled in a tiny English distillery and matured in English oak casks (ex-bourbon barrels or sherry casks are more what we have come to expect). English rum – whatever next?

Husband and wife team Paul and Jacine Rutasikwa are behind this. They have substantial landholdings in Matugga, some 13 miles north of Kampala, capital and largest city of Uganda. Sugar cane is grown there and molasses are extracted and then shipped to the UK, where Dr John Walters' English Spirit Distillery takes over.

The distillery was established in 2009, which makes it a veteran on the craft distilling scene. It is already noted for its small batch spirits and also makes Old Salt Rum. 'British rums with an East African heritage' they say, suggesting that this promotes 'East Africa's incredibly rich natural produce while showcasing British micro-distillery craft at its best'.

This is a very unusual product however and one which, I suspect, people will either greatly like or find really quite disagreeable. To my palate, it's smoky, with a burnt sugar taste that lingers rather too long, and the wood note from the uncharred oak casks is overly prominent. I expect you could cook with it, but at nearly £40 that's not a realistic option, so this is not a hit with me, I'm sorry to say, much as I wanted and tried to like it.

'*Pole pole ndio mwendo*' suggests the website, Swahili for 'slowly, slowly', which is great advice. But I just wish the Matugga team had taken note of their own sage counsel. This feels as if it needs further ageing to smooth off some of the raw edges and harsh notes.

And why not distil and age the spirit in Uganda, creating some local employment and providing a real provenance for the rum?

However, in the interests of balance, I should report that some online reviews have been positive, suggesting that this works well in a number of cocktails. Well, you might like to give this a try if looking for something a little out of the ordinary. It's certainly that.

58

MATUSALEM GRAN RESERVA

Brand owner: 1872 Holdings VOF
Website: www.matusalem.com
Origin: Dominican Republic

THERE'S MORE SPIN TO BE FOUND HERE THAN THE AVERAGE PARTY political broadcast. I got quite giddy trying to work it all out and eventually gave up in frustration.

This isn't to say that we don't have a decent enough product here, it's just that the marketing messages spread confusion and ambiguity. Take the bottle, for example, boldly embossed with 'Est. 1872'. Well, yes, there was a Matusalem company established in Cuba in 1872, but this was nationalised in 1959. Some local production continued but internationally the brand went into decline and, as so often, the different branches of the family fell to feuding amongst themselves. Eventually, after many lawyers had been enriched, the founder's great-grandson Dr Claudio Alvarez Salazar gained control of the trademark and relaunched Matusalem in 2002, using a distiller in the Dominican Republic. But 'Est. 2002' doesn't sound as impressive, so 130 further years of history were nonchantly pressed into service.

Then there's the label, with the dominant 15 numeral and the line 'Original Formula of Cuba'. That's pushing things just a little, I'd suggest. The 15 could easily be taken for an age statement (though I hastily acquit the company of trying to mislead) where, in fact, what we have is a solera process. And the Cuban claim – well, you've read the history, so decide for yourself. They would, in fact, have gone further if they could have done, but an attempt to register the phrase 'The Spirit of Cuba' was thrown out by the EU's General Court in June 2014. Cheeky!

Until very recently, this was produced under licence, but the ultimate owners, 1872 Holdings VOF (see, there's that 1872 again), have recently opened a spiffy new production facility in Monte Plata, Dominican Republic, said to be capable of producing more than half a million cases of rum annually. Apparently, the family's secret formula will continue to be used. A 'secret formula' – who knew?

As to the rum, well, it's agreeably smooth. There is a little bit of added sugar, I'd guess (and independent tests confirm this), but the balance is good, the mouthfeel soft and warming and there are honey, oak, spice, vanilla and banana and orange peel to find on the palate if you rummage about a bit. As I say, a decent enough product and reasonable value at £30–35. I'd suggest that you just ignore the somewhat spurious heritage messages and concentrate on what's in the bottle.

59

MEDFORD RUM

Brand owner: GrandTen Distilling
Website: www.grandten.com
Origin: USA

RUM WAS ONCE THE QUINTESSENTIAL DRINK OF AMERICA. IN FACT, by the end of the seventeenth century the hardy colonists pretty much relied on it. According to the traveller Edward Ward, writing in 1699, it was 'much ador'd by the American English [. . .] 'Tis held as the Comforter of their Souls, the Preserver of their Bodys, the Remover of their Cares, and Promoter of their Mirth; and is a Sovraign Remedy against the Grumbling of the Guts, a Kibe-hell [heel], or a Wounded Conscience.'

In fact, as many commentators have noted, with a reputed 150 or more distilleries in New England alone, importing 6.5 million gallons of molasses from the British West Indies, the 1764 Sugar Act, a measure to tax this vital ingredient, was deeply represented. 'No taxation without representation' and all that.

On his now legendary ride to warn of the arrival of the British troops, Paul Revere famously called in to see one Isaac Hall in his house in Medford, Massachusetts. Not a courtesy call, it turns out. Medford was by repute the home of the finest rum in New England and Hall was a distiller whose rum, according to H. F. Willkie, the brother of former presidential candidate Wendell Willkie, was strong enough to make 'a rabbit bite a bulldog'[6].

Anyway, however good the rum in Medford really was, it eventually gave way to bourbon and rye. Medford's last distillery closed in 1905 and the equipment was sold off during Prohibition. The rights to the brand name seem to have changed hands more than once, but this Medford Rum is today distilled by GrandTen Distilling of South Boston, one of the new wave of US craft distillers.

Like the Medford distillers of old, they employ pure blackstrap molasses, and work with wild New England yeast in an all-copper, small-batch still. The resulting spirit is matured in charred American white oak barrels and the wood influence is apparent, even suggestive of a lighter bourbon alongside dark brown sugar, vanilla and Keiller's Butterscotch (that dates me, because you can't get it anymore).

NB: No bulldogs were harmed in my testing of this product.

---

6 Quoted by Wayne Curtis, author of *And a Bottle of Rum: A History of the New World in Ten Cocktails*. Sadly, I have been unable to find the original reference. It's great, though, isn't it?

60

MEZAN PANAMA 2004

Brand owner: Mezan
Website: www.mezanrum.com
Origin: Panama

THOUGH IN FACT, THERE ARE LOTS OF THINGS IN THE MEZAN RANGE to interest the rum enthusiast here's one of real interest. I've picked the 2004 Panama release for no better reason than it is a) very affordable and b) there aren't very many Panamanian rums in the book and this is definitely one to showcase that country's distilling heritage. Needless to say, it's also very tasty.

Mezan is not a distillery but a bottler, based – well, it's not entirely clear where they are based, but the Caribbean is suggested. That's quite a lot of territory. According to their website, they have a Cellar Master possessed of a 'discerning eye' (one would have thought a discerning palate a better attribute, but we'll let that pass). Apparently, 'He tirelessly travels throughout the region, seeking out its hidden treasures: untouched rums, artfully crafted from a single year's distillation by a single distillery.' The Caribbean extends over 1 million square miles, so he's clearly a busy boy.

Stripped of the wondrous text of the spinmeisters, what this seems to mean is that Mezan are good at picking up casks of rum that have for one reason or another been overlooked and bottling them for our pleasure. What is to be commended is that all the rums they select and bottle are subject to three simple rules: they are unsweetened, uncoloured and only very lightly filtered.

Virtually all are the product of one single distillery, generally anonymous, though occasionally they offer a blended expression such as the Jamaican Rum Barrique XO. Importantly, they always make it quite clear what's in the bottle. If you're really interested and dig hard enough on the web you should be able to discover the source of the one that interests you. Or you can just go for it, enjoy the contents and speculate.

This is, in short, the real deal. Or so says my discerning palate, having enjoyed not just this fine Panama rum but Mezan's Guyana 2005, Jamaica 2005, Trinidad 2007 and the Jamaican Barrique XO. Snap up some of the Panamanian if you can, but if you can't don't worry. It's in the nature of limited bottlings like this that supplies will run out, but they are quickly replaced by something equally interesting and excellent value for money.

61

MOCAMBO 10 YEAR OLD

Brand owner: Licores Veracruz S. A. de C. V.
Website: www.licoresveracruz.com
Origin: Mexico

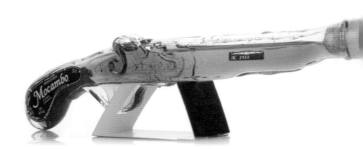

HERE WE ARE IN CÓRDOBA, A CITY WITHIN THE MEXICAN STATE OF Veracruz and the location of the signing of the Treaty of Córdoba (1821), recognising Mexico as an independent nation – though a reluctant Spanish government didn't acknowledge this for another 15 years. (Note to Editor and confused reader: Don't worry, the relevance of this will become apparent in a few paragraphs' time.)

Ron Mocambo is produced at the small, family-owned Licores Veracruz distillery in Veracruz. Natural yeasts are used to ferment the molasses and sugar cane juice in continuous column and pot stills respectively. After distillation, filtering and ageing in European white oak casks, the rum is bottled at the distillery, which also produces tequila, mescal, vodka and various liquors.

The range of rum produced by Licores Veracruz is actually quite extensive, but here in the UK we see primarily this ten-year-old Ron Mocambo in its unique buccaneer-pistol-shaped bottle (200 ml), though it does come in a boring old conventional bottle as well. There are white versions and other expressions and other labels because they make lots of rum here.

The glass pistol appears at first to be a bit of a novelty, but these oddly shaped bottles have their followers and I'd imagine would lend a certain retro charm to an *Only Fools and Horses* themed home bar. Some padded vinyl would complete the look.

But, actually, it would be a mistake to think of this merely as a naff curiosity, because the rum itself is perfectly agreeable and the pistol has local significance, being modelled on those used during the Mexican War of Independence. So, in Mexico at least, this is symbolic of the fight for liberation and national identity (I told you it was relevant).

As to the rum, remembering that if you pack the pistol you pay accordingly, it has a pleasantly sweet nose, lots of vanilla, spices, stewed fruit and a hint of liquorice on the notably dry finish. It has aged gracefully and is not at all dominated by wood notes.

There are better value rums out there, but allowing for the distinctive bottle, it's probably a worthwhile and fun purchase at least once.

62

MONYMUSK CLASSIC GOLD

Brand owner: National Rums of Jamaica
Website: www.monymuskrums.com
Origin: Jamaica

WE CAN'T REALLY HAVE A BOOK ABOUT RUM WITHOUT MENTIONING slavery somewhere. It is a topic well covered in historical texts and at The Rum Story in Whitehaven, but we have yet to touch on it here. Monymusk is as good a place to start, though it's hardly unique in its connection to the eighteenth-century slave trade, and similar stories may be found throughout the Caribbean.

The original Monymusk is in Aberdeenshire, but in 1755, the Grant family (still in residence in Scotland to this day) acquired extensive estates in Jamaica which were named after their home. Sir Archibald Grant owned a slaving station in West Africa, which provided labour for the Monymusk Estate in Jamaica where sugar cane was planted and rum distilled. Thankfully, the slaves have long since been freed, but the tradition of distilling rum continues.

For years, all of the rum was sold for blending and use in other brands. Today, there is a very large distillery on the estate, much of it funded by grants from the EU, producing a wide range of products. Much of the rum made here goes into Captain Morgan and Myers's Rum, their parent Diageo having an interest in the distillery.

However, following the EU investment in 2009, it was decided to market a small range of rums under the estate label – hence Monymusk. These comprise a blend of pot and column still rums which, along with long fermentation and the absence of chill filtration prior to bottling, gives the Monymusk expressions their distinctive character.

Classic Gold, part way up the range, is a great place to start. It's light and easy to drink, yet holds its own in mixed drinks. On serving a glass, I got a huge and rather lovely blast of ripe bananas, followed by a veritable cocktail of fruit and floral notes. On the palate there's a great balance of sweet and spicy notes and the mouthfeel is refined and surprisingly subtle, with a somewhat dry and rather moreish finish. It's definitely one with which to surprise a friend who 'doesn't like rum' (we've all got one) and change their mind.

Typically found in specialist stockists for around £30 or less, the straightforward packaging disguises a rum of considerable pedigree and quality.

63

MOUNT GAY XO

Brand owner: Rémy Cointreau
Website: www.mountgayrum.com
Origin: Barbados

THERE IS, AS WE HAVE NOTED, A MAJOR DIVIDE IN THE WORLD OF rum, between those producers who add some sugar to their spirit immediately prior to bottling and those who do not. Mount Gay are firmly in the unsugared camp. That's not simply because the regulations in Barbados prohibit any additives, but because the company themselves are adamantly opposed to it.

So, in tasting any of their ranges, your palate has to be prepared for a drier style. Though Barbados was first settled by the British, the Mount Gay brand is today owned by the French Rémy Cointreau and this is reflected in the more austere style and the naming of the different expressions.

There are two cheaper rums from Mount Gay (Eclipse and Black Barrel) and very tasty they are, but I'd suggest spending a few pounds more on this XO. For around a fiver more than the Black Barrel you get a well-matured and robust rum, with a higher proportion of pot distilled spirit. The components in the blend range from seven to 15 years old and this additional age adds great richness to both the nose and the palate.

This is really quite a sophisticated product, perhaps best suited to sipping to allow the distinctive dry notes of cedar wood, old leather and dark preserved fruits to come to the fore. Master Blender Allen Smith is responsible for the cask selection and the blend of pot and column distilled spirit that goes into the final bottling.

His reputation as one of the Caribbean's most highly regarded blenders has been built on products such as the XO, though his skills really stand out with signature expressions such as the rare 1703 (see the following entry).

Though far from the only distillery on the island (Malibu is also made on Barbados, but that's the last time that particular brand will be mentioned), Mount Gay is one of the largest and its products enjoy some of the widest international distribution.

They also run a polished visitor centre and it is possible to take a variety of tours to see the production and ageing processes. With tourism a vital part of the island economy, the distillery is a popular visitor destination.

64

MOUNT GAY 1703

Brand owner: Rémy Cointreau
Website: www.mountgayrum.com
Origin: Barbados

DISTILLERIES, ESPECIALLY THEIR MARKETING TEAMS, TEND TO GET very excited about history, and Mount Gay is no exception. But perhaps we can forgive them, because this Barbadian distillery has the distinction of being the birthplace of rum.

Established in 1703 – you didn't think they'd picked the date at random, did you? – the first distillery went through a number of owners until one John Sober brought in Sir John Gay Alleyne, another Barbadian of immortal memory, to manage the estate. He introduced new strains of cane, improved crop yield and enhanced the production process – innovations so significant that on his death in 1801, Sober named the estate for him. Good thing, too: Mount Sober wouldn't really work as a brand name.

I have an unwritten rule to avoid any bottles with a three-figure price tag and I'm afraid that this does just break that barrier. It is, one must admit, a lot of money for a bottle of anything but, as it says on the bottle, it has been 'perfected by tradition' – who could argue with that?

Mount Gay 1703 has been blended from the distillery's oldest stocks, with rums aged between ten and 30 years. The extra age of this mature spirit takes the XO style up a level, with greater intensity, complexity and depth of flavour.

The distillery talks of oak, toffee and leather, with ripe banana, candied fruits and soft spices. Hard to disagree with any of that, and I would add a hint of a barbequed pineapple and traces of the elusive and highly desirable *rancio*, a marker of distinguished old cognac that I was excited to find here.

Supplies are necessarily limited due to the shortage of aged spirit of a high enough quality, and only around 12,000 bottles are released annually. You may have to look a little harder to find a bottle without breaking the bank, but the effort will be richly rewarded by a superstar rum experience.

It's said that Mount Gay's Master Blender Allen Smith tried 44 different blends before he was completely satisfied with the final product. He's done all the hard work; you simply have to open your wallet, then sit back and enjoy. Oh, and try to stay completely sober.

65

MYERS'S RUM
ORIGINAL DARK

Brand owner: Diageo
Website: www.myersrum.com
Origin: Jamaica

ANOTHER OF DIAGEO'S SECONDARY RUM BRANDS, THIS IS AN OLD-fashioned standard that is stocked the world over and was a cocktail classic long before rum became trendy. The label proudly claims it to be 'World Famous' and, here at least, that's not just marketing hyperbole. Myers's was long a favourite amongst British service personnel, being a standard in NAAFI stores wherever our forces were to be found, and is fondly remembered as offering great value and guaranteed good times!

The company was originally founded by a Jewish family with trading links to the Royal Navy. Fred L. Myers launched the brand in 1879; it was (according to the Diageo website) then launched in the USA in 1934 and eventually acquired by Seagrams. Subsequently, in the non-stop process of consolidation that characterises the global spirits industry, it has ended up with Diageo, who have had the good sense to leave it largely alone. The label and the rum both now possess a retro charm which lends it vital credibility in a world of johnny-come-lately rums with more or less spurious heritage credentials.

It's produced in Jamaica, blending the production of nine different molasses-based continuous and pot still distillations and then matured for up to four years in white oak barrels. As you might expect, it's heavy, slightly smoky and quite bitter (in a good way), with a powerful treacly aroma that bursts out of the glass as you pour. But this is not where this rum shines, unless you are an old squaddie or matelot set on recapturing the flavours of your misspent youth in the service of the Crown.

No, the intense Myers's flavour belongs in cocktails, most famously the Planter's Punch. Fred Myers invented this, may his name live forever, terming it the 'Old Plantation Formula'. This isn't a cocktail book, but this is a classic, so here goes: one measure sour (lime juice); two sweet (sugar syrup); three strong (rum – I'd suggest Myers's Dark, funnily enough) and four weak (water). Some folk add a dash or two of Angostura bitters. Orange makes a great garnish. Serve, enjoy and repeat.

Myers's still offers great value, even if no longer available at NAAFI prices. It's perfectly possible to pick up a bottle for less than £20 and that's a lot of flavour and tradition for your money.

66

NEGRITA

Brand owner: La Martiniquaise
Website: www.bardinet.fr
Origin: Blend

ARE YOU OFFENDED BY THE PICTURE OF THE WOMAN ON THE BOTTLE or find the image culturally insensitive? It certainly awakens difficult cultural and historical associations and understandably, some people do, which may be why this rum, remarkably popular in France, Spain, Finland and a number of African markets, is hardly seen either here or in the USA.

However, Negrita (a term of endearment in Central and South America but carrying uncomfortable associations for English speakers) is marketed as cheerful and accessible and the brand is one of a select few rums selling over one million cases annually. Considering that that has been achieved without the major US market, clearly something is going right though, were it to be launched today it would certainly be under a new label.

Her picture first appeared in the 1880s when Paul Bardinet, a young producer of liqueurs in Limoges, France began experimenting with the crude cane sugar alcohol then known as tafia, ageing it and experimenting with different blends. The girl with the ribbons became known as 'La Negrita' and a legend was born.

Bardinet's family firm developed the spirit, initially using rums from Martinique in the Caribbean and Réunion in the Pacific Ocean (both French colonies). Today, the blend is exclusively Caribbean and based on pure sugar cane but, in the international expressions at least, it also includes some molasses-derived spirit.

You can find it easily in French supermarkets at very competitive prices, so it's one to consider if you ever holiday there. Despite the modest price and simple packaging, it's a versatile product that can be drunk neat or in a range of cocktails.

In Cambodia, apparently, it is sold in pharmacies and drug stores, and is drunk by women after giving birth in order to 're-energise' them! Full disclosure: I can neither confirm nor deny the efficacy of this and, obviously, have no personal experience in the matter – though I may have had a few drinks after my own children were born. Purely for ceremonial reasons, of course.

67

NEW DAWN 18 YEAR OLD

Brand owner: New Dawn Traders
Website: www.newdawntraders.com
Origin: Dominican Republic

I MUST ADMIT I WAS A LITTLE CONCERNED BY THE NAME NEW DAWN. It seemed a little cultish, and I imagined some messianic figure holed up in a Central American jungle clearing, awaiting the arrival of a spaceship full of aliens destined to save the world – or at least the true believers.

And the New Dawn people do actually have a mission to save the world. They point out that in our interconnected yet atomised global economy nearly everything that we own or consume has spent part of its life in a huge anonymised container ship, invisible for much of its life, travelling a vast network of international trade routes, calling in at massive, largely mechanised ports of which we know or care little. Today, an ultra-large container vessel (ULCV) can carry more than 20,000 individual containers, stretch over a quarter of a mile in length and weigh 210,000 tonnes. That's a big ship, carrying a humongous lot of stuff.

Though they bring us lots of cheap things, you don't have to be Sir David Attenborough to realise that such behemoths are not without problems. New Dawn are trying to do something about this by reverting to sail. It is, as they admit, something of a symbolic gesture to restore a human scale to the international food trade, but one which requires us to confront our own consumerism at a conscious level.

Right now they sell fine Caribbean rum and chocolate made from sail-shipped cargo, brought across the Atlantic by the Fairtransport brigantine, *Tres Hombres*. Eventually they aim to operate their own sailing ship.

I liked the New Dawn rum, which is from Santo Domingo in the Dominican Republic, where it was blended at Oliver & Oliver. Its journey continued across the Atlantic aboard the *Tres Hombres*, where it spent a further month and a half on the rolling seas. The rum was then blended with Cornish spring water and bottled in a local brewery. There were 870 bottles.

Of course, it's probably all gone by now, but that's not the point. I wanted you to know about these guys so that you can try what else they've got. It'll be good and your conscience will be clear.

68

OLD MONK 7 YEAR OLD

Brand owner: Mohan Meakin Ltd
Website: None
Origin: India

DO MY EYES DECEIVE ME? SURELY WHAT WE HAVE HERE IS A BOTTLE of Grand Old Parr, a venerable brand of blended Scotch whisky much favoured in Colombia and indeed parts of the USA.

Well, no. In fact, I have been taken in by the remarkable resemblance of this once incredibly popular Indian rum to one of Diageo's lesser-known whiskies. However, it's unlikely that you would ever confuse the products, as this is unashamedly a molasses monster that in its heyday was the classic Indian 'go to'. Like so much in India, the company behind Old Monk has its roots in the British Raj, but is today a thoroughly Indian concern. The Brits did, however, leave behind a local taste for distilled spirits.

It's important to grasp that great lakes of whisky and rum are distilled and drunk in India. The volumes are unimaginably large by Western standards and we get all the more confused by the fact that much Indian 'whisky' would be classified as rum here in Europe. But within the huge Indian spirits market, Old Monk was once a colossus, selling close to eight million cases annually in the early 2000s. Since then, sales have plunged, and competitors such as McDowell's No. 1 Celebration have left it labouring sadly behind.

Old Monk is now seen as an old man's drink, which is a shame, for this is indeed a genuine rum and not adulterated (according to European definitions) as so many Indian spirits can be. First developed in 1954, its incredible success was built almost entirely through word of mouth and a particular association with the Indian military. However, despite falling sales, the company seems curiously reluctant to promote the brand.

It probably won't be to everyone's taste. This is robust, full-flavoured stuff, designed to pack a punch (bottled at an eccentric 42.8% strength, just to add to the fun) and which definitely will appeal to old-school rum drinkers brought up on Navy rum styles, despite never having been within several thousand miles of the Caribbean.

Rumours persist that owners Mohan Meakin will throw in the towel and discontinue production. These appear regularly on Indian social media and, just as regularly, are energetically denied. But the sales trend has to be reversed soon or this particular monk will find himself a very lonely anchorite indeed. Let us pray it is not so.

69

OLD PORT

Brand owner: Amrut Distilleries Private Ltd
Website: www.amrutdistilleries.com
Origin: India

INDIAN DISTILLER AMRUT — IT TRANSLATES AS 'NECTAR OF THE gods', always a good sign — was a pioneer following the country's independence in 1947. Under the British Raj, a substantial distilling industry had been established, but Amrut was one of the first to be founded under Indian ownership. Initially a relatively modest concern, based in Bangalore and serving local markets, the company has now grown significantly and has built an international reputation for its Indian single malt whiskies.

Unlike many domestic Indian 'whiskies' which are based on molasses, sometimes with the addition of a percentage of Scotch whisky (shipped there in bulk), Amrut's premium single malt whiskies meet international quality standards and have been well received on world markets, winning a number of prestigious awards. However, volumes are relatively small compared to the company's other products (Indian whiskies, brandies and rum).

India is a significant producer of high quality sugar cane, so against that background it's little surprise that Amrut's Old Port is a marvellous maelstrom of moody molasses set against a surprisingly fruity backdrop (I wasn't expecting tinned lychees on the palate but there they were). Though not widely available in the UK, it is attractively priced and you should, with a little bit of work, be able to track down a bottle for just over £20, making it extraordinarily good value. It's far from the most complex rum you'll encounter but its smooth, fruity notes will prove a trusty companion to your favourite mixer over some ice.

Note, though, the all-important word on the label: 'Deluxe'. There is a cheaper version, of limited appeal to the Western palate from what I can gather, and while this might save you a few rupees, one gathers that it is something of a false economy. The 'deluxe' descriptor is something of a relative term, but it is the version of Old Port that you should look for.

Given Amrut's success with single malt whisky, and the dynamism of both the company and the overall Indian economy, it would not be a surprise to see more premium rums from this stable. Clearly the distilling and marketing skills are there, so this may well be one to watch in years to come.

70

OPTHIMUS 18

Brand owner: Oliver & Oliver International Inc.
Website: www.oliveryoliver.com
Origin: Blend

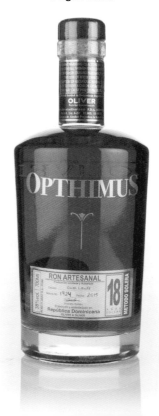

CUBA CAN'T HAVE BEEN ANY FUN IN THE EARLY 1960S IF YOU WERE on the wrong side of Fidel Castro and his mates. Property was nationalised and many business people fled the island. The best-known exiles are the Bacardí family, but they were far from alone in abandoning their homes and livelihoods at the point of a gun.

The island had known earlier waves of turmoil, most notably at the end of Cuba's struggle for independence from Spain in the late nineteenth century. Caught up in this were a Spanish family, the Olivers, who had established their business in Cuba when Juanillo Oliver turned from Spanish soldier to Cuban distiller in 1874. However, by 1898, another war had broken out and Cuban revolutionaries burnt down the family farm and distillery. The Oliver family eventually left the island in 1963.

Thirty years later, however, Pedro Ramón López Oliver, a descendant of the founder, visited Cuba and was able to recover many original family records concerning the production of their rums. This visit inspired a new business, which was established in the Dominican Republic in 1993 as a rum blender. It is this Oliver & Oliver that brings us the Opthimus range, as well as a number of other brands and private label bottlings.

Opthimus 18 (remember this is a solera statement, not aged like Scotch whisky) is around the middle of the range and provides a great entry point to the Oliver rums. This one is soft and beguiling, with a smooth and gentle entry from the lush, fruity nose. The various blends are made up of rums from across Central America and the Caribbean, including casks from Panama, Guatemala, Nicaragua and the Dominican Republic as well as Trinidad and Tobago and other distilleries in the French and English West Indies. They then age and blend the different distillates, placing them to mature in Tempranillo and bourbon barrels under the traditional solera method, and additionally offer port-cask-finished rum.

This is classy stuff, though frustratingly bottled at 38%. With a retail price exceeding £50, this is a super-premium offering by rum's standards and it would be nice to have the opportunity to try this at a somewhat higher strength. Still, I can conclude with the words of another Oliver: 'Please, sir, I want some more.'

71

PAMPERO ANIVERSARIO

Brand owner: Diageo
Website: www.pampero.com
Origin: Venezuela

THIS COMES IN A SQUAT LITTLE BOTTLE THAT LOOKS IDEAL FOR making a Molotov cocktail and is wrapped in a leather pouch – perfect for storing your matches. (NB: The Editor suggests that you do not try this at home!)

The brand also has a TV commercial with horses running down a deserted shopping street and bravely saddled by some photogenic young people. It is uncannily reminiscent of the Guinness Compton Cowboys of South Central Los Angeles with their horses. Some coincidence surely, and nothing whatsoever to do with the fact that both brands are owned by Diageo. Thinking about it, a rum chaser might go very well with a pint of Guinness. But do not try this at home either, because the brand's signature serve – a 'taste of carnival' apparently – is, wait for it, Pampero and cola. I hope that's radical enough for you.

Pampero, you see, is all about 'freedom and passion' (*groan*), for Pampero represents the new Llaneros – the Venezuelan cowboys who helped liberate various South American countries from Spanish colonisers – and the brand makes much of the innovative spirit of its 1938 founders who pioneered ageing. There's even a llanero and horse stamped into the wax seal on the bottle and, as we all know, if it's on a wax seal it must be true.

This expression was first released in 1963 to commemorate the company's 25th anniversary. Back then, the company was still fully independent, joining the group which today we know as Diageo in 1991. The base is locally grown sugar cane, and the distillery uses three different distillation processes.

After initial distillation, the alcohol can be made 'lighter' or 'heavier' by undergoing its second and third distillations in a column or pot still. Aniversario is, I believe, a blend of both column and pot still rums, subsequently aged for up to four years in casks previously used for maturing whisky or sherry.

Perhaps influenced by the packaging, I had no great hopes for this, but was pleasantly surprised by its weight, range of flavour and sweet/dry balance. More in hope than expectation, I did actually try it with ice and cola and it came through with flying colours though as a general rule I would keep it for sipping.

72

PENNY BLUE VSOP

Brand owner: The Indian Ocean Rum Company
Website: www.pennybluerum.com
Origin: Mauritius

THE EXOTIC-SOUNDING INDIAN OCEAN RUM COMPANY IS A JOINT
venture between the Medine Distillery of Mauritius and the long-
established London wine merchants Berry Bros & Rudd , purveyor
of rare vintages to the nobility and gentry.

They have a wonderful shop and cellars at 3 St James's Street in
Mayfair, where they have been trading continuously since 1698 and
where you can find all kinds of wonderful wines and spirits. And you
don't have to belong to the upper classes to drop in, as they welcome
the hoi polloi with as generous a smile as the aristocracy. In fact,
I've heard that some of their customers actually went to grammar
school, though they do make them pay cash. This is entirely unfair on
BB&R, who are very, very nice people, so just ignore that.

If you do go – and you absolutely should – then when you're not
gazing at the antique weighing machine, which has measured princes,
poets, popinjays, politicians and even plutocrats from Pakistan, you
can feast your eyes on a very special selection of carefully selected
spirits. It's a very lovely shop, with lovely things.

Many of these are considerable bargains. I could mention some of
their private label whiskies, the No. 3 London Dry Gin and the
quirky King's Ginger liqueur (in fact, I appear to have done so), but
the Penny Blue rums really stand out for a combination of quality
and value for money that's hard to beat.

There are three in the range, but for the entry level, I give you this
VSOP expression. Like its stablemates, it is bottled at natural colour
and non-chill filtered. Distilled from sugar cane in a four-column
continuous still, it is then aged in casks that have previously held
cognac, bourbon and Scotch whisky. After around four years ageing,
Medine's Master Distiller Jean-Francois Koenig and Doug McIvor
from Berry Bros & Rudd take over and blend the final batch, which
is bottled in Mauritius.

Initially, it may well strike you as rather dry, especially if you are more
accustomed to a sweeter Caribbean style (there is no added sugar
here). But give it time: fruitier notes will come to the fore and the
vanilla, cedar wood and spice of the casks becomes apparent.

And, yes, it is named after the rare postage stamp.

73

PIRATE'S GROG NO. 13

Brand owner: Pirate's Grog Rum Ltd
Website: www.piratesgrogrum.com
Origin: Not disclosed

SHIVER ME TIMBERS, SHIPMATES. APART FROM ONE WELL-KNOWN brand, I'D rather imagined that the pirate and rum link had walked the plank of dodgy PR, but it seems that it is still a thing.

That, at least, would seem to be the conclusion of the Hackney-based 'boutique rum company' behind Pirate's Grog (and I had fondly imagined that the only pirates in Hackney were buy-to-let landlords). But it's all rather confusing: a quick glance at their website might lead you to the conclusion that it was distilled on the island of Roatán, off Honduras. That's strange, because according to other independent sources, there isn't actually a distillery on Honduras. Do we detect villainy afoot here?

Further investigation suggests that Pirate's Grog founders Gareth and Beth Noble were house-sitting on Roatán when they met Dutchman Robert J. van der Weg who was doing something unspecified with rum. All three began working together, launching their products in the UK in 2014. The rums are said to come from 'neighbouring distilleries' (as they would have to, really) and the entry-level Pirate's Grog expression is a vatting of Caribbean rums, aged for between three and five years in American oak ex-bourbon barrels. Disappointingly it's bottled at 37.5% but seems to be intended more for party cocktails than serious, considered drinking.

Judging by the website, a major activity for the Pirate's Grog folks is running pop-up rum bars at food and drink shows, music festivals or private and corporate events. They do seem to like a good pirate-themed fancy dress party. There's nothing at all wrong with that, but having taken a look around, I decided I probably wouldn't bother covering their efforts. And then I had the good fortune to taste their No. 13 in one of those cleverly presented little samples from the Master of Malt people.

This No. 13 is a different beast and doesn't need any swashbuckling Spanish Main nonsense to convince you of its considerable merits. This is a single cask 13-year-old rum from 'Central America' (big place), rather nicely presented in bottle and tube. For the presentation, age and quality, it's decent value, if you can find some for your pieces of eight (or 70 quid). My advice: ignore the confused and confusing presentation, cast all the pirate stuff overboard and simply concentrate on the yo-ho-ho. (Sorry.)

74

PLANTATION XO
20TH ANNIVERSARY

Brand owner: Maison Ferrand
Website: www.plantationrum.com
Origin: Barbados

YOU ARE GOING TO BE SO VERY GLAD THAT YOU BOUGHT THIS BOOK. Because you bought this book, you now know about Plantation Rum and their outstandingly good XO 20th Anniversary edition, which is something really special; a treat for any discriminating drinker (which, of course, you most certainly are). It will convince anyone – anyone – that top-class rum is one of the glories of the world of spirits. And you can share freely it in the noble pursuit of educating your benighted friends, because if you shop around, you won't need to pay quite £50 for a bottle. And if said friends know anything about great spirits, they will think you paid a lot more, especially when you reveal, with theatrical flourish, the splendid bottle.

What a dignified container! Such poise, distinction and grace, hinting at the magificence within. Do the contents disappoint? Tush! Of course the contents do not disappoint. The owner of Maison Ferrand, a noted cognac house that also makes great gin, is Alexandre Gabriel, and this XO release marks his 20 years as rum blender. Nothing but the finest expressions would do justice to such a moment, and Gabriel, artisan businessman and tireless entrepreneur, is a true obsessive, driven by his personal search for perfection in spirits.

Plantation do not distil. Instead, they work with partners in the Caribbean and Central America to source special casks. After a few years in the Caribbean, the rum is then transported to the Château de Bonbonnet in the heart of Charente, France, where it is further aged in French oak, and the casks, as Gabriel says, are 'nurtured like children' in carefully controlled cellars[7]. Unusually, this involves a technique known as 'petites eaux' in which a small quantity of water that has first been held in old rum casks is slowly added to prevent excess evaporation and gently bring the spirit down to bottling strength (in this case 40%). It's a painstaking process.

The XO 20th Anniversary is an 'assemblage' (or blend) of fine rums between 12 and 20 years old, all originating from Barbados, a crucible of rum production. Many different types of casks are used for ageing, ranging from new white oak to bourbon barrels as well as cognac casks, each with different levels of toasting.

Smooth, sophisticated and well-balanced – just like the discriminating readers of this book.

---

7   This may be a French thing. If you nurture your children in a cellar here it will end badly for all concerned.

75

STIGGINS' FANCY
PLANTATION PINEAPPLE

Brand owner: Maison Ferrand
Website: www.plantationrum.com
Origin: Barbados

'HE WAS A PRIM-FACED, RED-NOSED MAN, WITH A LONG, THIN countenance, and a semi-rattlesnake sort of eye—rather sharp, but decidedly bad,' writes Charles Dickens of the Reverend Mr Stiggins, a Nonconformist minister, whom we find enjoying a drink with a somewhat florid and well-padded female (the landlady, Mrs Weller) in *The Pickwick Papers*.

'Beside him stood a glass of reeking hot pine-apple rum-and-water, with a slice of lemon in it; and every time the red-nosed man stopped to bring the round of toast to his eye, with the view of ascertaining how it got on, he imbibed a drop or two of the hot pine-apple rum-and-water, and smiled upon the rather stout lady, as she blew the fire.'

Stiggins' red nose rather suggests – as Dickens intends – that the 'decidedly bad' reverend gentleman was somewhat too fond of the demon drink, which, as a Nonconformist, he should of course have completely abjured. Naughty Reverend Mr Stiggins.

But thank you too, because this passing reference to a Victorian delicacy and a disreputable cleric inspired US drinks writer Dave Wondrich and Maison Ferrand's Alexandre Gabriel to create this remarkable product. Initially intended to be a one-off, it was presented to delegates at the bibulous Tales of the Cocktail 2016 event in New Orleans. But it was declared Best New Spirit at the show and could not be allowed to die. Fittingly, the Reverend Mr Stiggins appears on the label, his features based on an 1867 illustration. Immortalised on a bottle of rum – what larks!

To make Stiggins' Fancy Plantation Pineapple, actual pineapples are peeled by hand and the rinds infused with Plantation 3 Stars rum which is then redistilled. Separately, the flesh of the peeled fruits is infused for three months in Plantation Original Dark rum and the two liquids married together and then rested in oak for a further three months.

Praise Jesus! This is absurdly tasty. What's more, it is ridiculously cheap, around £35 which, when you consider it, can hardly cover the work involved, let alone acknowledge the inspired decision to recreate this yummy treat. Drink it neat, drink it over ice, drink it as a toddy with lemon, but drink it you must, all the while singing a hymn of praise to Charles Dickens, to the rum-soaked Reverend Mr Stiggins (red nose and all) and to the iconoclastic duo who have brought us this delicious libation.

76

EL RON PROHIBIDO

Brand owner: Fraternity Spirits
Website: www.fraternityspirits.com
Origin: Mexico

THE FIRST THING THAT CATCHES THE EYE ABOUT THIS IS THE unusual flask-shaped bottle with the handle on the neck, and then the ornate, somewhat antiquated label. It sounds rather cheesy, but despite my innate cynicism I thought it actually worked quite well, reminding me of the kind of little-known, artisanal product you pick up somewhere obscure and bring home in triumph to impress your mates. El Ron Prohibido – 'Prohibited Rum' – sounds promising, too, with its tantalising hint of the clandestine and forbidden. If nothing else, that will impress your chums.

As the great Sir Thomas Dewar, whisky magnate, once proclaimed (about Prohibition, so the reference is entirely apt), 'If you forbid a man to do a thing, you will add the joy of piracy and the zest of smuggling to his life'. Disappointingly, on reverting to the web to check the exact wording, I found this sage advice attributed to the American philosopher Elbert Hubbard who may, it seems, have coined other aphorisms that we think of as 'Dewarisms'. Perhaps Tommy was quoting him.

Anyway, equally disappointingly, no one is trying to stop you enjoying this Mexican rum, if that is your pleasure. The 'prohibido' bit refers to the eighteenth-century Spanish monarch King Felipe V of Borbón who apparently issued an edict against the Mexican rum then known as *Chinguirito*. This had been filled into barrels used to bring sweet wine from Spain and during the lengthy return trip back home the rum had absorbed the aromatic characteristics of the barrels, resulting in a high-quality product, which the grateful citizenry then enjoyed rather too well. Or so the story goes.

Today, as it's not really prohibited at all, your only problem will be availability. While this is supposedly distributed in the UK, stocks appear to be only patchily available. That's a shame, because while some will not care for the bitter initial taste, I find that it grows on you, and in a world of somewhat over-sweetened products offers a genuine point of difference. It is further distinguished, according to the distillery, by 'adding a touch of raisin wine', though whether that's at the start or end of the blending isn't clear.

The prominent 12 on the label refers to the claimed age of the solera, so is perhaps best regarded for its contribution to the packaging aesthetic. Well worth tracking down, though not to everyone's taste.

77

PUSSER'S 15

Brand owner: Pusser's Rum Ltd
Website: www.pussersrum.com
Origin: Guyana

THE 'PUSSER', AS YOU PROBABLY KNOW, WAS THE SAILOR'S TERM FOR the Purser – the officer in the Royal Navy who, until 31 July 1970 issued the famous rum ration on board Her Majesty's ships. Though it started in 1655 as a twice-daily issue of half a pint, by 1970 it had been reduced to just 90ml of high-strength rum – which is nearly four standard pub measures, so quite enough, you might think, for the chaps (no ladies at sea until 1990) operating large warships. Or even the small ones. The Admiralty agreed, and so on Black Tot Day a great naval tradition came to an abrupt end.

Navy Rum was quite unique, being distilled in the world's only surviving wooden pot stills (they have a body of Guyanese greenheart, a hardwood, and copper necks) in Guyana. While other rums are still produced in these remarkable pieces of equipment, only Pusser's can claim that their product is produced to the original Admiralty standard and officially licensed as such. Being over 250 years old, the wood is now thoroughly impregnated with a unique combination of esters and congeners – organic compounds that impart the notably heavy-bodied, very flavourful and deeply aromatic flavours found here.

Then the spirit is aged for 15 years – ancient by rum standards – and so this is actually quite the bargain, for the combination of history, taste and maturity. But how, you ask, has this come to pass if the rum ration was abolished nearly 50 years ago? For that we must thank former US Marine Charles Tobias, who pestered the Admiralty to reveal the secrets of its production so that he could offer the public the chance to taste real Navy Rum.

It took him ten years to get their agreement and launch the brand, but in 1980 it was available once again. Incidentally, Pusser's pay a royalty to Navy charities, and in acknowledgement of this and his work in reviving Navy Rum, Tobias was eventually awarded the MBE. Quite right, too. But if your heart yearns for the actual rum the Navy drank, you can look to the Black Tot Last Consignment (for a mere £650 – see entry 18).

The 54.5% ABV Gunpowder Proof is a pretty heady throwback to naval tradition – something of a dreadnought amongst rums. Apparently, you could wet gunpowder with this and the stuff would still explode. Needless to say, don't try that at home (and especially not on board ship).

78

R. L. SEALE'S 10 YEAR OLD

Brand owner: R. L. Seale & Co Ltd
Website: www.rumsixtysix.com
Origin: Barbados

YOU'RE ENTITLED TO EXPECT THAT WHEN A CHAP PUTS HIS NAME on the bottle – and bottles his rum in such a rum looking bottle – that it's going to be good. This does not disappoint.

Richard Seale is a third-generation distiller, known for his acerbic commentary on the rest of the industry; the opinions are presented with good humour but he does have very definite views on how rum should be made. If you know whisky, think of Mark Reynier and you've got the idea. I listened to Richard speak at the annual London RumFest (well worth it; you should go next time) and learned more during his presentation than I had done in days of research.

As essential background, know that R. L. Seale's 10 Year Old Rum is produced by Richard at the Foursquare Distillery in Barbados, founded in 1926 by his great-grandfather Reginald Leon Seale. I guess that just adds to the pressure of putting the family name out there, though he seems to thrive on the pressure.

You should also know that he's not at all keen on adding sugar to rum (this is an understatement, by the way) and he's a great advocate of traditional pot still producers. 'Rum was not always a poor man's drink,' he told us (a useful reminder), adding, 'But industrial production has wiped out small-scale production.' He duly presented some rather depressing statistics on the loss of distilleries in Jamaica. At the end of the nineteenth century there were 148 distilleries; today there are but four.

But I soon cheered up after trying some of his very fine products. 'Sweetened rums sell an illusion,' says Richard and, as he's not in the fairytale business, be prepared for an uncompromisingly dry and spicy initial impact as you sip this ten-year-old style. The first notes are promising, and then it just gets better and better, unfolding as it goes. Eventually you're going to find notes of banana, melon, almond and oak along with suggestions of greater age – especially the elusive leathery, woody, dusty note the French call *rancio*, which is greatly admired in well-aged spirits.

Bearing in mind that once you have drunk the contents, which you will do quite quickly, you've got a very funky lamp base, which alone is a wee bit of a bargain at a typical UK retail price of around £40.

79

RELICARIO

Brand owner: Beveland Distillers
Website: www.relicariorum.com
Origin: Dominican Republic

THIS HANDSOME FELLOW IN A SMART PRESENTATION WITH A HEAVY glass bottle and wood effect closure would grace any back bar. Relicario comes from the Dominican Republic, the larger part of the island once known as Hispaniola (Haiti accounts for the remainder of the land mass), in the very heart of the Spanish Main.

So, it hails from a country with serious rum credentials, but do the contents live up to the packaging? Well, from the very first taste, I'd have to say so. Though it's hard to find out very much about the product, or exactly where it's distilled, I'd rate it (in the vernacular of the west of Scotland) as 'a wee cracker'.

If you know the Scottish delicacy known as black bun, you might recognise some of the fruity notes that emerge from the bottle, along with mouth-watering hints of pastry. In fact, the standard black bun recipe calls for a small measure of whisky; may I be forgiven in Forfar and pardoned in Paisley, but I'd go so far as to suggest that replacing that spirit with a 'wee drappie' of Relicario would result in an utterly delicious confection.

If you're a lover of the classic spicy and fruity style of rum then this is going to work very well for you, both as a delightful sipping rum but with enough weight and body not to be submerged in a cocktail. It's not the most complex rum you'll ever encounter but it certainly won't disappoint even the most fastidious connoisseur.

Relicario is produced using a solera system, with a blend of six to ten-year-old spirit (the premium version, Supremo, uses rums of up to 15 years, all from ex-bourbon American white oak casks). With a parent company based in northern Spain, distribution has historically been concentrated in western Europe and the Czech Republic, but supplies are steadily finding their way to UK specialists, where you should be able to find a bottle for around £30–£35.

Given some promotional support and a bit of luck, there seems to be no reason at all why this won't find favour with British drinkers who will appreciate its well-mannered taste and dapper presentation.

80

RON CUBAY AÑEJO

Brand owner: Corporación Cuba Ron SA
Website: www.roncubay.co.uk
Origin: Cuba

RON CUBAY WAS FIRST DISTILLED IN 1964, WHEN CUBA WAS resolutely hitched to Soviet Communism, so probably served to take everyone's mind off the infamous Missile Crisis, which had taken place less than two years previously. Until relatively recently you could only find this in Cuba, where it had been restricted exclusively to domestic sales but supplies have been available in Europe for the last five years or so.

The distillery is at Santo Domingo, Villa Clara, in the centre of the island. Government-backed producer Corporación Cuba Ron are also behind the better-known Havana Club, which is a joint venture with Pernod Ricard.

While there are apparently five varied expressions of Ron Cubay available in Cuba, we in Europe see just three: a three-year-old Carta Blanca; this Añejo and the Añejo Reserva Especial, reputedly seven and ten years old respectively, all column still produced and a blend of various strains and ages.

However, only the eldest in the family arrives at 40%, while its two siblings are bottled at 38% – a drop in strength that always disappoints when studying the label, and induces some scepticism even before tasting. The saving in duty is relatively trivial and I would always prefer a higher strength bottling (I'm partial to 46%) that I can dilute to taste rather than this skinnier version. However, I'm sure they have their reasons.

Perhaps I should have tasted this blind, but with the 38% strength in mind, it seemed a little light in both body and mouthfeel. In fairness, that made for an agreeable sipping rum that was dangerously easy to drink and seemed well balanced across the sweet fruity palate with hints of coffee and fudge in the background. It also mixes well, so high marks there.

The lower strength clearly contributes to the modest sub-£25 price point, but you should find the equivalent Havana Club expression at a pound or so less which would likely be my call.

On the other hand, were you to visit Cuba this would probably be the one to drink, just to get into the rhythm of the place. *Viva la revolución* – or then again, perhaps not so much.

81

RON DE JEREMY

Brand owner: One Eyed Spirits
Website: www.rondejeremy.com
Origin: Blend

FINNISH MAY BE THE FINEST LANGUAGE IN THE WORLD. THEY HAVE *nousuhumala*, to describe the feeling of getting pleasantly drunk at the start of the evening, and *laskuhumala* for later, when you just want to fight or vomit. But I have discovered the best Finnish word: *kalsarikännit* – which means to get drunk at home in your underpants, with no intention of doing anything else.

Now what rum would you drink at home in your budgie smugglers? Why, Ron de Jeremy of course, named for and promoted by legendary 80s porn star Ron 'The Hedgehog' Jeremy, veteran of more than 2,000 adult movies. The rum is dedicated to Ron for no better reason than two wacky Finns with a brand agency realised that 'rum' in Spanish is 'ron', and the most famous Ron they could call to mind was the man with the mighty member. So they called him up and Ron de Jeremy was born.

Now that might seem just a flippant and gimmicky idea (which actually, it was) but these are Finnish people and so they take everything, especially their fun, quite seriously. Having aroused Ron they then called the best rum maker they could find and set to work. With their rum consultant they took off to Panama (and I thought writing was a tough gig) to meet the renowned rum-maker Francisco 'Don Pancho' Fernandez, who created Ron de Jeremy for them using rums from Barbados, Trinidad, Jamaica and Guyana.

A label was then created, featuring Ron looking uncannily like a moody Che Guevara, and the product launched. Helpfully, within days of its Canadian release, the Manitoba Liquor Control Commission promptly banned it on the grounds of indecency, generating much press coverage and, predictably, lots of sales. Then Valvira, the Finnish government agency in charge of alcohol legislation, decreed that Ron could not appear on the label as the branding 'may lead to sex and alcoholism'. Love those funky Finns.

Thing is, it's actually a very tasty drop of the old kill-devil (as rum was once known). You may eschew porn movies in favour of *The Sound of Music*, but still enjoy the nice balance of sweet fruit, spices, sugar cane and oak that characterise this well-made rum. Great value too, at a little over £30, and guaranteed to be a talking point at any party. Finally, please note that I have avoided any smutty double-entendres in Ron's entry (oops).

82

RUMBULLION! XO
15 YEAR OLD

Brand owner: Atom Brands
Website: www.ableforths.com/rumbullion
Origin: Blend

WELL, SOMEONE HAD TO. SOMEONE HAD TO TAKE RUM'S ORIGINAL name – well, one of them anyway – and apply it to a modern-day brand. The wonder is that we've waited from the middle of the seventeenth-century until today for rumbullion to reappear in our drinking lexicon. As far as we know, it originally meant the tumult or uproar that might be associated with rumbustious behaviour in a public house. Just fancy that.

There are three versions of these puppies, and this is the big dog: a base of Caribbean rum, laced with orange peel, vanilla pods, spices and some cane sugar. In the wrong hands, that could have been something of a dog's breakfast, ending up a syrupy, sticky, sick whippersnapper that would quickly sate even the sweetest toothed and least discriminating drinker.

Not here. This is rather cleverly done, taking the Rumbullion original onwards and upwards by using a 15-year-old base that adds depth and complexity to the original recipe. Less, as they say, is more, and by exercising some restraint with the various added flavourings, the Rumbullion blender has created a surprisingly complex and rewarding dram.

Note that the pack, in its simple brown paper wrap, is the smaller 50 cl size, so this retails at the equivalent of more than £80 for a standard (70cl) bottle. However, on the positive side, the rum is 15 years old and the 46.2% ABV strength adds some punch, ensuring that this stands up well to an ice cube or three. The maker's recommendation is to mix with red vermouth and an orange twist to create a novel take on the Palmetto cocktail (top tip: for best results use decent quality vermouth and really treat yourself).

Atom Brands, who are behind this marvellous concoction, form part of the group that includes the Master of Malt online drinks retailer, so this seems as good as place as any to sing their praises as a cornucopia of keenly priced beverages. You will find everything from the commonplace to the most arcane and obscure ambrosial tinctures that your heart could possibly desire. For many of the products on offer it's possible to obtain a little sample (3cl) before you commit to the full bottle. Apart from easing the pressure on your wallet, it's a great way to try 101 different drinks, were such a quixotic notion ever to cross your mind.

83

RYOMA 7 YEARS

Brand owner: Kikusui Shuzo Company
Website: www.cellartrends.co.uk/spirits/ryoma.php
Origin: Japan

JAPANESE RUM — IT'S NOT WHAT YOU EXPECT, IS IT? I WAS REALLY quite excited to discover this, and the minimalist packaging and dark glass further piqued my interest. Japan is much better known for its whiskies, so while the distilling skills and tradition are there, rum comes as a surprise.

Ryoma 7 Year Old Japanese Rum is made at the Kikusui Distillery, in the south of the archipelago on the island of Shikoku, some 180 miles to the south-west of Osaka. The region around the village of Kuroshio, where the distillery can be found, is known as the oldest, and once the largest, producer of sugar cane in Japan. The rum itself is named after Sakamoto Ryōma, a prominent Japanese figure in the movement to overthrow the Tokugawa shogunate in the nineteenth century, a time when Japan was opening, often reluctantly, to the Western influence which Sakamoto favoured.

Ryoma is made very much in the style of a rhum agricole, typical of the French-speaking Caribbean, made from freshly pressed sugar cane rather than the more common molasses base. Indeed, Ryoma is marketed in France, where the style is more familiar to a market comfortable with the pale colour and dry initial taste.

The distillery itself is a field-to-bottle operation, thus guaranteeing quality by controlling the entire production process, from planting the sugar cane to bottling the rum. The sugar cane is harvested in November and December when, despite the southern location, it can be very cold.

After the cane is cut, it is pressed and then boiled to a concentrate, which is fermented, distilled and stored for ageing in white oak. There are no additives or caramel and the liquid is accordingly pale, despite its age, and the rum itself is lighter, more fragrant and drier in style than you may expect.

The UK distributor suggest that it offers rum connoisseurs ready for a new rum experience 'an outstanding premium sipping rum', and recommend mixing it with lime and sparkling water or even enjoying it with hot water. At over £50, it's not an everyday purchase, but if you like the agricole style and are looking for something intriguing and very different, you may just have found it. Kampai!

84

SAILOR JERRY

Brand owner: William Grant & Sons
Website: www.sailorjerry.com
Origin: Blend

THERE WAS ONCE A TIME WHEN SPORTING A TATTOO WAS A SIGN OF your iconoclastic attitude, a reflection of your radical, devil-may-care approach to life. A tattoo marked you out as a rebel. Or possibly a convict or a sailor.

In that great tradition, Norman Keith Collins ('Sailor Jerry', to his friends) worked in Honolulu's Chinatown in the 1960s. He is regarded by cognoscenti of the tattooist's art as a legendary figure, and remains influential to this day. Collins died in 1973.

Through a somewhat tortuous process, details of which continue to be disputed, rights to his name and designs passed out of the family and third parties established a merchandise business in 1999 selling Sailor Jerry products. Curiously, enough, tattooing was becoming fashionable by then; no longer the mark of the outsider, a tattoo was considered cool, hip and edgy. There was money to be made from Jerry's legacy.

One of those products licensed by the Sailor Jerry company was a spiced rum, which is today owned and marketed by William Grant & Sons, the folks behind Glenfiddich, The Balvenie, Hendrick's Gin and many other fine drinks brands. Now, hardcore rum enthusiasts look askance at spiced rums, regarding them with some disdain, but I can't say that I take such a militant, purist line: it's your money and if you enjoy this kind of thing, then live and let live is my view. It's meant to be a fun product, so lighten up.

It's a rather unsubtle wee drop though, heavy on the vanilla and cinnamon, though thankfully not too saccharine. The original version was considerably sweeter, and despite the fact that the recipe was changed as long ago as 2010, people still bang on about this on the web. Apparently, if you liked the earlier version, the nearest equivalent available today is Admiral Vernon's Old Gold. I wouldn't know: eventually you have to move on.

I haven't got a tattoo either. They've become a tedious cliché, and with Samantha Cameron and Felicity Kendal sporting them I fear the game is up. Even bank managers have them, which is hard on the average brand ambassador (sorry, brand ambassadors and mixologists, but was that really the message you thought you were sending?).

85

SAJOUS

Brand owner: Michel Sajous, Chello Distillery
Website: www.thespiritofhaiti.com
Origin: Haiti

YOU WANT HANDCRAFTED? ARTISANAL? THEN LOOK NO FURTHER. And, in all likelihood, look away, because this really is an acquired taste and you probably won't like it!

Sajous is a clairin, the principal native product of Haiti (though Barbancourt is also from Haiti, we should be clear that it is a very sophisticated rum indeed). Clairin is probably best thought of as a primitive version of rhum agricole as we know it today, but again, just to be clear, that's 'primitive' meaning 'early'.

There are claimed to be more than 530 tiny clairin distilleries on Haiti, often operating in the middle of the sugar cane fields. Fermentation relies on natural yeasts and all the distillery operations are undertaken by manual labour. Organically grown sugar cane is concentrated to a syrup, which is then stored, thus allowing year-round production. Because marketing and packaging have made little impact on Haitian society, much of the volume is sold in bulk: consumers simply bring a container to the retailer and have it filled – much like a Victorian 'jug and bottle' shop.

It is bottled straight off the still, which will have been fired by *bagasse*, the ground-up remains of the pressed canes, at around 50% ABV. Clairin would remain largely unknown in the West were it not for the enthusiasm of Italy's Luca Gargano, dedicated rum enthusiast and importer to Europe of some very distinctive products.

It's probable, let's be honest, that European consumers would find most clairin unpalatable (totally undrinkable, in fact, unless you have a taste for bootleg moonshine) but a Triple A protocol has been developed in an attempt to grade the products and to help bring some of the higher quality expressions to European markets.

One that may be found in the UK is Clairin Sajous, product of the Chello distillery, owned by Michel Sajous. But be warned: if you have never tasted any new make from any distillery, this will come as a shock. And, if you have, this will still come as a shock! This is forceful stuff: raw, elemental and packed with strange and exotic notes, not all of them pleasant. You may not care for the reek of putrefying vegetation, for example. But get past it, drop your preconceptions and think of this as part of your rum education. It was certainly part of mine. Or, as an alternative, try Boukman (entry 21).

86

SANTIAGO DE CUBA
CARTA BLANCA

Brand owner: Corporación Cuba Ron SA
Website: www.cubaron.com
Origin: Cuba

YOU CAN GET AS FAR AS THE MAIN DOOR OF THE DISTILLERY HERE, and even taste the rum at an adjacent bar, but that's as far as you will get (believe me, I've tried) until things change pretty drastically in Cuba. Whoever manages the distillery – presumably employees of some Cuban-government-controlled affair – are pretty touchy about access to the distillery (there isn't any) and don't even like you taking photographs of the exterior. There is a small and rather dilapidated rum museum in the city but it is scarce consolation for missing out on the real thing. Goodness knows what they're so worried about.

Santiago – Cuba's second city – could, however, be a place of pilgrimage for rum enthusiasts, partly because a great deal of Cuban rum flows from here but mainly because the distillery is the site of the original Bacardí distillery, home of the bat. Don Facundo Bacardí and his family started distilling rum nearby in 1862 but subsequently built this distillery. They lived and worked in Santiago until the company was nationalised by the Cuban state in 1959 following the revolution and all the family's property was seized. There is an argument that the family's defiance in the face of this setback is what propelled them from being a regional brewer and distiller to today's global force but, not surprisingly, they tend not to see events in those terms. For their part, the authorities have largely airbrushed Bacardí from Cuban rum history.

Anyway, this Santiago distillery – said to produce nine million litres annually, though I have been unable to verify this – produces an extensive range of brands, including Ron Caney, Ron Santiago de Cuba and Ron Varadero, offered at a range of ages. Cuban rum can be quite confusing as, apart from Havana Club (the sales of which are controlled by Pernod Ricard), the producers are little engaged with such capitalistic concepts as brands and marketing.

Consequently, information is somewhat sparse on Santiago de Cuba rum. This Carta Blanca is molasses-based, aged in oak for up to three years but then filtered to strip out the resulting colour. In theory, most of the flavour remains, but the filtration process, combined with the 38% bottling strength, seems to me to have enervated the product. It remains a pleasant, if light-bodied, white rum perhaps best employed in cocktails – the Mojito is the classic, but remember to discard the stems from your mint!

87

SMITH & CROSS

Brand owner: Hayman Distillers
Website: www.hayman-distillers.co.uk
Origin: Jamaica

Let's not. Let's look harder. 'Traditional Jamaica Rum', it says. And then, in smaller print, 'Pure Pot Still', 'Navy Strength 57%'. Things are looking up. And what is this? The shelf sticker reads £36. Quick, grab a bottle before they spot the mistake.

Thing is, it isn't a mistake (thank you, and would the marketing folks step away from the bottle before they bling this up and hike the price). This is a bottle full of history; arguably a little time capsule from before the arrival of the multi-column still and consequent advent of industrially produced light rums. This is anything but light and as a result has had quite an impact in the more purist end of the cocktail bar world where authentic, intense flavours are prized.

Produced using a combination of the molasses, skimmings, cane juice and syrup bottoms from sugar production, and the dunder of the previous rum production, then fermented with indigenous wild yeasts, this speaks of its Jamaican roots with a basso profundo. Think a young Harry Belafonte delivering the 'Banana Boat Song' – a good place to start thinking about the ripe notes of cooked bananas that serenade you from the glass before the molasses hit home along with the decaying pineapple (trust me, you'll love it), sultanas and dark Oxford marmalade. This is so good you could spread it on your toast.

Though bottled in England, it's distilled on Jamaica's Hampden Estate, renowned as a producer of heavy pot still rums with a high ester content; a style that would have been familiar in the nineteenth century and first half of the twentieth, but which subsequently fell somewhat out of favour.

The Smith & Cross name reflects London's heritage of sugar and spirits production: they once operated a sugar refinery in London's Docklands and traded in rum and other spirits from their extensive Thames-side warehouses.

Today the name belongs to another noted family firm, Hayman Distillers, better known for their excellent gins. So the brand is in very good hands and we may hope for further interesting releases before long. I suppose I should end on a warning note: if you're used to Bacardi's Carta Blanca, say, you'll find this a bit of a shock. This is a cask-strength Laphroaig compared to a bottle of Bell's, so look out!

88

SPARROW'S PREMIUM

Brand owner: St Vincent Distillers Ltd
Website: www.sunsetrum.com
Origin: St Vincent

I'm not really sure what 'premium' means. Actually, I don't think anyone really does. For many brands, a sub-£25 retail price would be their entry-level expression. Certainly, Sparrow's standard tall round bottle and screw cap has all the style and presence of a supermarket own-label product and hardly generates expectations of high quality.

Reputedly, it was named for Captain Jack Sparrow from the *Pirates of the Caribbean* movie franchise following the filming of *The Curse of the Black Pearl* on St Vincent. But how time flies: rather alarmingly, I looked that up to find that it was released in 2003. This doesn't have the look of a licensed product, though. If it was, it would be a great deal ritzier and a lot more expensive.

So, it's carrying the name of a fictional character in a fantasy film about imaginary pirates who probably didn't drink rum anyway. There's a cross-cultural mash-up for you.

But never mind, because the good folks at St Vincent Distillers have pulled off a very tasty drop. From a molasses base and using traditional column stills (as opposed to the modern multi-column still) this is aged up to seven years. Sparrow's initially hits some very spicy top notes but drinks as a rather more subtle and delicate rum than the nose or price would lead you to expect.

It was a category winner in the 2017 World Rum Awards which leads me to the conclusion that, tasted blind, the underlying quality of Sparrow's can be appreciated free from the preconceptions that its basic packaging might generate. That leads on to the further conclusion that what we have here represents very fair value that more discerning rum drinkers will be happy to discover.

There is actually quite a lot of history here which would allow the distiller to reposition this product and charge a real premium. The distillery was established in the early 1900s, when it was known as Mount Bentinck, working the molasses from a nearby sugar mill. The proprietors have changed over the years, but since 1996 it has been in independent private ownership, and the facilities have been expanded and modernised. *Pirates of the Caribbean* feels like the movie franchise that never dies, so perhaps a super-premium Sparrow's sequel will follow.

89

ST AUBIN WHITE AGRICULTURAL RUM 1819

Brand owner: Saint Aubin Ltée
Website: www.rhumsaintaubin.com
Origin: Mauritius

LOCATED ON THE ISLAND OF MAURITIUS, ST AUBIN STYLES ITSELF as 'the artisanal distillery'. If you want to check it out, they are open to visitors and you can visit their 'live eco museum' and eat in their elegant restaurant.

As you might expect from the strong French influence, the distillery makes much of its terroir. 'Varietal cane selection combined with the perfect exposure of our fields and the volcanic nature of our soils' they say 'go into the making of an excellent "terroir"'.

Sugar has been grown here since 1819, but while the company expanded in the production of tea, and speciality sugars, rum production is relatively new. Today, there are two stills here – a small, traditional pot still surmounted by a short column and a more modern single column continuous still. With such varied apparatus, a wide variety of rums are produced, including dated vintages, flavoured and aged rums and liqueurs. My pick from their extensive range is the White Agricultural Rum, distilled from 'fangourin', the pure sugar cane juice of Mauritius.

The rhum agricole blanc is available at two strengths (40% and 50%) and is a very fine example of this style. As the label proudly proclaims, only the heart of the distillation ('coeur de chauffe') makes it to the bottling line and the result is authentic, intense and potent, especially at the higher strength. On the initial impact, the nose is grassy, floral and slightly vegetal with a hint of vanilla pods and cardamom. To taste, the typical grassy notes of rhum agricole dominate and the finish is dry, spicy and agreeably hot.

This expression is not aged in wood, thus the spirit is direct and immediate, leaving a clean and fresh impression on the palate, though fading quite quickly. Even at 50%, it is pleasant to take neat, but would add an unexpected note to classic cocktails.

The brand is relatively unknown in the UK but is available in good specialists. At under £30 it represents good value if you want to explore the agricole style. Differing so dramatically from the taste of a molasses-based rum, this will not be to everyone's taste, but this is a classic of its type that has not gone unnoticed in major international competitions.

90

ST BARTH CHIC

Brand owner: R. St Barth
Website: www.rhumstbarth.com
Origin: Guadeloupe

ST BARTH RHUM, FROM THE FRENCH CARIBBEAN ISLAND OF ST Barthélemy, is the creation of French international footballer Mikaël Silvestre (a star for Arsenal then Manchester United, and World Cup finalist for France in 2006). I knew there had to be something better in life for retired footballers than flogging cheap crisps, so I'm happy for Mikaël, especially as the brand represents his memories of his blissful childhood and family holidays.

There are three expressions in the range, but the easiest to find will be Chic, a four-year-old rhum agricole. 'Easiest' is a relative term, as a mere 5,000 bottles are released annually and I'd anticipate most of those going to France. Some may be found in the UK if you put your mind to it, and you may even turn up one of the 2,000 bottles of the Authentique, a well-aged drop if ever I've tasted one.

However, Chic is what concerns us here. Until recently they maintained that it is 'particularly appreciated by knowledgeable female consumers' and, just in case you were in any doubt about that, the company's website still goes on to insist that 'the sweetness in the Bourbon finish makes this variety easier to taste, particularly for a female drinker'. What patronising guff.

I don't see why the ladies should have all the fun anyway, and as I don't see anything particularly feminine (whatever that may mean) about the product, I propose to tell you about it.

St Barthélemy itself is actually a rather chic island, though on investigation, it would seem that the sugar cane is grown and the rum distilled and bottled on nearby Guadeloupe. Everyone is rather coy about exactly which distillery is behind this, so essentially this is a labelling and marketing exercise.

I really don't know why. I'd be shouting about it, because it's a very tasty, classic rhum agricole with a bourbon spin. Keeping shtum in a world of growing transparency and openness seems like an own goal, so that's a red card for Mikaël, even if his excellent Chic would triumph in many a penalty shoot-out.

This seems to have launched in the UK at over £90, which is silly. However, as we go to press, it appears on a well-known specialist's website at a few pennies under £46. He shoots – he scores!

91

SAINT JAMES
FLEUR DE CANNE

Brand owner: La Martiniquaise
Website: www.saintjames-rum.com
Origin: Martinique

DESPITE THE ENGLISH-SOUNDING NAME, HERE WE HAVE A VERY French rhum agricole from Martinique, another from the giant La Martiniquaise company. Apparently, it was originally named St Jacques, but sometime in the eighteenth century the anglicised version was adopted by the company founder, the Reverend Father Edmund Lefebure, Superior of the Convent of the Brothers of Charity, in order to help sales in the British colonies in North America. There was a healthy market for rum there which makes it all the more ironic that today it is sold mainly in France.

This Fleur de Canne style, a healthy 50% showstopper, is white rum made exclusively from sugar cane, giving it rich and sugary flavours whilst clearly showing the vegetal note that distinguishes the agricole style. Though the cane is grown on the company's own plantations, these are located on the more humid eastern side of Martinique, adjacent to the mountains. Fleur de Canne ('Flower of the Cane') is made only during very dry seasons, as the stress causes the roots of the plant to grow more tightly packed, contributing to a very specific flavour unobtainable in any other way.

The distillery was modernized in 2010, working primarily columns stills. As you would expect, it holds the AOC accreditation from Martinique, but the company's history is proudly displayed in an adjacent museum and visitor centre. Amongst their claim to fame is the assertion that St James was the first spirit to employ a square bottle, reputedly to avoid breakage in the ships' holds and minimize the space between the bottles when packed (so eat your heart out, Johnnie Walker!).

None of this makes the slightest difference to your drinking pleasure today, of course. I wouldn't drink this neat but it works in a simple Ti Punch with brown cane sugar syrup and a lime wedge, or makes a beefy Planter's Punch, thanks to the higher alcohol content.

Note, however, that to the palate unaccustomed to style this may be something of an acquired taste. I'm not going to reproduce some of the tasting notes that I found online – suffice it to say that they were less than complimentary.

But ignore the critics: if you can get hold of some of this Fleur de Canne (find a friend in France), it's an inexpensive introduction to a classic style.

92

SAINT JAMES CUVÉE 1765

Brand owner: La Martiniquaise
Website: www.saintjames-rum.com
Origin: Martinique

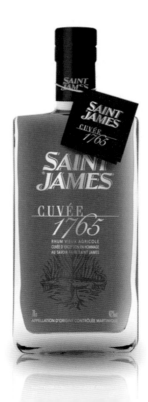

BY WAY OF CONTRAST WITH THE FLEUR DE CANNE, HERE'S A MATURE rhum agricole from the same Saint James' stable in Martinique. Though little seen in the UK, it's a massive operation and a very significant player in the important French market. In fact, Saint James is the bestselling agricole rhum in the world; has long been well regarded and appears in a number of early cocktail books.

Huge prestige was attached to the launch of this expression in 2015, as it marked the 250th anniversary of the distillery's foundation and was in homage to what is believed to be the original style and recipe. Aged a minimum of five years in a combination of French or American small oak casks, it's a roasty, toasty spicy drop with suggestions of dark bitter chocolate. There was no real surprise when it collected gold medals in competitions for the aged agricole style.

Cuvée 1765 is the creation of master blender Myriam Bredas and oenologist Marc Sassier, who selected six vintages that together attempt to recreate the style and flavours of the product that they consider would have been made back then. I suspect that they are probably flattering their predecessors, because I rather doubt anything this sophisticated was released back then, but that's our good fortune. Some things are just better today.

Actually, we Brits would not have been terribly welcome in 1765, having just given the French a severe (and well-deserved) spanking during the Seven Years' War. Back in France the notorious La Bête du Gévaudan, reputedly a wolf-like monster, was terrorising the Auvergne and south Dordogne, killing up to 100 people a year (look this up; great story) and the British parliament had just passed the Stamp Act, which led, more or less, to the American War of Independence (we lost).

Like many of the rums from La Martiniquaise, the Cuvée 1765 is excellent value if you care for a drier, spicier rum. Perhaps because the French market for rum is significantly larger than in the UK, and rather more competitive, not to mention the considerably more favourable tax regime for spirits in France, this is a fixture on good French *cavistes'* shelves at around €50 or less. But the brand tell me that they are actively looking for a UK distributor, so there is some hope that at least some of the products in the extensive Saint James range may eventually find their way here.

93

TAKAMAKA EXTRA NOIR

Brand owner: Trois Frères Distillery
Website: www.takamakarum.com
Origin: Seychelles

ESTABLISHED AS RECENTLY AS 2002, TROIS FRÈRES IS THE ONLY commercial distillery on the Seychelles so, it just seemed churlish to leave them out. (A fermented cane juice beverage known locally as 'baka' is also made here but you would search in vain for it outside the islands.)

I learned that the Seychelles actually comprises 115 different islands situated almost in the middle of the Indian Ocean. The distillery is located on Mahé, the main island, and was established by the local d'Offay family on the site of an old tropical spice plantation, La Plaine St André, which dates back to the 1700s and today distils locally grown sugar cane. Proprietors Robert and Diana d'Offay have three sons, hence the 'trois fréres' name, though the distillery is better known as Takamaka, after a local bay and type of tree.

As you'd expect, it's on quite a small scale, with two small pot stills and a rectifying column, but an extensive range of different rums and rum spirit aperitifs (lower strength) are also produced. Though sugar cane is the main source for the rum, some molasses are also used.

This Extra Noir is the distillery's most recent product, described as 'a blend of our three years old aged sugar cane juice distillate and molasses distillate rums' and, as they freely admit, containing added caramel to give it the extra dark colour.

Locally it is bottled at 43% but the export version has been dropped to 38%, like so many others. It's cheap enough, but I'd rather they reverted to the higher strength and dropped the colouring so we could see what we were paying for. I think that would work better as the market develops.

As things stand, it's a pleasant enough if largely unmemorable rum. There is a slight burnt sugar note, but overall the experience is unexceptional one way or the other. I'd imagine that nothing could be nicer if you were on holiday in the Seychelles than visiting the distillery to enjoy a tour and a couple of cocktails. I'm all for local enterprise and initiative but, as you will have deduced from this somewhat truncated entry, try as I might, I really couldn't get too excited about this.

94

DIAMOND DISTILLERY
13 YEAR OLD

Brand owner: That Boutique-y Rum Company
Website: www.thatboutiqueyrumcompany.com
Origin: Guyana

THAT BOUTIQUE-Y RUM COMPANY. SOUNDS A BIT LIKE THAT
Boutique-y Gin Company doesn't it? And rather like That
Boutique-y Whisky Company as well, come to think about it. There's
a reason (thank goodness it wasn't blind chance – that would have
been worrying).

They're all part of the same group, fired by the mission to track down
interesting, small parcels of unusual spirits (rum, gin, whisky – you
work it out) and bottle them in handy half-litre bottles with funky,
hand-drawn labels featuring some reference to well-known drinks
industry characters. Or even, if on occasion they get desperate, me. I
appear on one of their whiskies and a rather tasty gin.

Now they have launched a rum company and my spies tell me
they will be offering a number of very special limited bottlings
from distilleries that the true rum enthusiast needs to get to know.
Coming up are rums from Foursquare and Monymusk, amongst
others. But, because I've featured something from both of those, let
me concentrate on this cracking 56.1% ABV 13 Year Old pot still rum
from the Diamond Distillery in Guyana.

As I explain in the entries for El Dorado, Pusser's and Wood's,
Diamond is a remarkable and very special place. Amongst other
things, it's home to the last *wooden* stills in the world. This bottling is
of rum from the Versailles single pot still which, over the years, has
been moved from its original home at Versailles on the west bank of
the Demerara River, via the great historic sugar estates of Enmore
and Uitvlugt to its present home at Diamond, where it works to
this day. It's a historical anachronism, but a living, breathing one
that gives us a powerful suggestion of exactly how the rum of our
forefathers may have tasted.

I'd like to say that they don't make rum like this anymore. Mostly,
they don't, but they do at Diamond, obviously. Nowhere else has
quite this extraordinary combination of location, heritage, ancient
technology and distilling expertise, so full marks to the folks at That
Boutique-y Rum Company for sniffing out this and other tasty treats
for our delectation. Surprisingly delicate and light in colour despite
its strength and age, this is a rum to sip and savour.

Inevitably, however, supplies are limited, but if this has run out do try
their other offerings. There's something there that you'll like.

95

THE DUPPY SHARE

Brand owner: The Westbourne Drinks Co.
Website: www.theduppyshare.com
Origin: Blend

LAUNCHED IN JULY 2014, THIS IS A NON-AGED BLEND OF JAMAICAN and Barbadian rums from two of the best-known and most highly regarded Caribbean distilleries: Worthy Park Estate (Jamaica) and Foursquare of Barbados, which is covered in detail in a number of entries. But they didn't create this, for The Duppy Share is blended and bottled in London by relative newcomers to the drinks industry, set up by an ex-Innocent Drinks team. What smoothies!

The duppies are, apparently, distant relatives of the distillery angels who take their share of Scotland's finest. These malevolent spirits or ghosts originate from Jamaica and swoop between the islands of the Caribbean, stealing the best part of the maturing rums, as well as getting up to other kinds of mischief.

Said to be 'spirit masters, skilled in the fine art of blending' the duppies take only the finest rums. Or so it says on the website, so it must be entirely beyond question.

But if this is what they picked I think they may have had a bit of an off day. It's not that it's nasty or undrinkable – far from it – but it is far from the smoothest, most subtle or complex rum you're ever going to find.

Having said that, if you want something that lends a bit of weight and some spicy flavour to your favourite rum cocktail then this may do the job, though there are others more competitively priced and not so assertively fiery. It seems to me that the more robust Jamaican flavour dominates here, making the blend somewhat unbalanced. Maybe that was the mischievous duppies' side.

To be fair, it's not outrageously expensive and they do offer a little 20 cl bottle if you want to try it before committing to the full £30. And, to their credit, there are no games with the strength, as this is bottled at the standard 40%. I should add that the label is quite cheerful and distinctive, if you like that kind of thing.

Ian Fleming, who had a house on Jamaica which he greatly loved (Goldeneye – hence the movie title), briefly mentions the duppy in his second novel, *Live and Let Die* (1954), mainly written at the house.

Actually, I think that's really all I want to say about this.

96

TILAMBIC 151 OVERPROOF

Brand owner: Tilambic Rum Ltd
Website: www.greenislandrum.com
Origin: Mauritius

HERE'S ANOTHER MIGHTY OVERPROOF RUM YOU MIGHT WANT TO consider. But, apart from the 151 proof strength (75.5% and thus nearly 53 UK units of alcohol per bottle – that'll last you for nearly a month according to the UK Chief Medical Officer's guidelines), there's actually more to this than meets your watering eyes.

'Tilambic' is apparently the local Creole name for moonshine and for the small pot still originally used by villagers to make rums for domestic consumption. However, as the label makes clear, that's all changed. Today the romantically named International Distillers (Mauritius) Ltd, a company dating to the 1960s, runs a modern 30-foot tall column still and uses molasses as the base for the spirit – so nothing particularly noteworthy there. It's not actually sold in Mauritius and appears to be an exclusive production for the UK.

But things get interesting after that. Astonishingly, it's actually aged. Not just for a few weeks or months, or even a year or two, but for 'up to seven years', according to the producers. That's genuinely unusual and something that makes this big Mauritian bruiser stand out from the crowd. Better still, it's not been chill filtered and there's no added sugar or colouring, so you taste a completely unadulterated product that's packed with authentic flavour derived from the spirit and the American oak ex-bourbon casks. What's more, the warehouse is temperature controlled to provide a nice even maturation and the result is a lovely golden colour, a surprisingly delicate nose (once the initial alcohol vapour has evaporated) and a more complex set of flavours than you might reasonably expect.

As an experiment, I left some in a glass for several days. My office filled with a delightful fruity aroma and the rum itself remained exceptionally tasty.

The point, of course, is not to slam this down in shots. You could, I suppose, but that's just silly and adolescent and rather a waste, not to mention actually dangerous (you could wake up with a tattoo, or do yourself considerably worse damage). The options then are to dilute to taste, serve over ice and let the melting rocks do the work, or employ this in a cocktail where you actually want to taste the rum.

However, at the risk of sounding like some sanctimonious health-and-safety killjoy, try to stick to one, please. That way, the bottle might actually last a month and you considerably longer.

97

TROIS RIVIÈRES CUVÉE DE L'OCÉAN

Brand owner: Bellonie et Bourdillon Successeurs
Website: www.plantationtroisrivieres.com
Origin: Martinique

LIKE SO MANY OTHERS, THE NOTED TROIS RIVIÈRES DISTILLERY IN Martinique was founded on the site of a sugar plantation. Production of spirits there can be dated to the 1780s, though only began in earnest in 1905. The distillery's reputation amongst lovers of the agricole style has grown consistently since its products began to be more widely distributed from 1980. At the same time, production was greatly expanded with the purchase of a second column still. Today, distillation follows the Appellation d'Origine Contrôlée rules.

Though the production of Trois Rivières was moved to Rivière-Pilote in 2004 by new owners, the precious original distillation column was rebuilt on the new site and continues in operation. A considerable range of rums are offered, including rare vintages dating back to 1953.

Just as a point of interest, a well-known Scotch single malt noted for its comparatively modest pricing currently offers its 1953 vintage distillation for a little under £9,000 (which, by the way, is roughly the price of a brand new Ford Ka+), whereas you can still find, if you're lucky, bottles of the 1953 Trois Rivières for less than £1,500. If this book sells well, I'm very seriously considering splashing out.

However, most of their offerings are more modest, and for the price of a tank of petrol for the aforesaid automobile you can get this rather interesting Cuvée de l'Océan expression, made with sugar cane grown in fields very close to the sea on Martinique's south coast, adding a subtle briny aroma to the resulting spirit which is, of course, unaged. It's said that the cane's high sugar content results from being grown in clay soils that are rich in magnesium, whilst their roots 'bathe in sea water'.

Like its fellow islander Saint James Fleur de Canne, this deceptively light-bodied rum serves very well in the classic Ti Punch. The simplest of drinks, requiring only rum, lime and some sugar, it effectively demonstrates the old adage that less is more.

The slightly salty note lends a teasing ambiguity and there is complexity enough here to engage the connoisseur while slipping down easily. As the Cuvée de l'Océan is bottled at 42%, it carries more weight than is first apparent. However, if that's not enough for you, the distillery does also offer their blanc style at 50% and a mighty 55%.

98

WATSON'S DEMERARA AND TRAWLER RUMS

Brand owner: Ian MacLeod Distillers
Website: www.ianmacleod.com
Origin: Guyana/Blend

WE'RE GOING TO LOOK AT THIS PAIR TOGETHER (THINK OF IT AS A BOGOF bonus – that's supermarket-speak for 'Buy One Get One Free') because this is rum as it used to be in the last century and because they are hard to find outside Scotland. But keep reading . . .

In the Scotland of my youth (*very* last century) it wasn't unknown to see discarded empty quarter bottles of Watson's Demerara or Trawler Rum lying in the gutter in the less salubrious parts of Leith (don't ask what I was doing there). I'm not going to say that rum was a downmarket drink, but I can't imagine that very much was served at Gleneagles or in the North British Hotel (what The Balmoral was called in the last century).

But, back when we still had a fishing fleet of any account, it was indeed a popular call in the bars of Scotland's east coast fishing towns and villages and, for consumption at home, a particular favourite of old ladies when served as rum and pep. That's alcoholic peppermint cordial, by the way, not a well-known cola drink. Try it if you want, but it's perhaps best thought of as an acquired taste. Mainly acquired by old ladies with moustaches.

But don't look down on these brands because of their history. Try to ignore the basic packaging (it helps if you think of it as ironically retro in style). Remember that bearded people with tattoos were drinking this long before beards and tattoos became de rigueur in hipster circles. Then take a look at the price. You'll get change from a twenty-pound note and you will have just picked up something of a bargain.

Sure, these aren't the most sophisticated rums you'll ever try, but they are a lot better than you think they're going to be and they deserve better exposure and distribution.

In style, the Trawler is the somewhat drier of the two, with a slight bitterness about it that will divide opinion. It's a blend of Guyanese and Barbadian rums, whereas the Demerara expression is 100% Guyanese. Personally, it's my favourite of the two – it's a little sweeter but with a satisfying complexity on the palate if you let the taste linger. Just try them (pep optional) – you may be pleasantly surprised.

99

WOOD'S OLD NAVY RUM

Brand owner: William Grant & Sons
Website: www.williamgrant.com
Origin: Guyana

IT'S BIG, IT'S BOLD AND IT'S A BARGAIN. WHAT'S NOT TO LIKE? WELL, the new packaging for one thing. This well-loved old brand had a major makeover in April 2016. The objective, apparently, was to 'make the Wood's bottle and packaging more premium, iconic and memorable'. Marketing speak: dontcha just love it?

The salty old tars who make up the principal audience certainly noticed and weren't slow to train their big guns on the new look. 'Makes it look like a Chinese rip off' was one of the milder comments, so we'll have to hope that they get over it without moving on. Maybe it will appeal to Hoxton hipsters, though I have my doubts.

But the contents remain uncompromisingly traditional and utterly delicious – though a little goes a long way. This is old-school rum from the Royal Navy tradition. If I were the captain of a 'dirty British coaster with a salt-caked smokestack, butting through the Channel in the mad March days' I'd want a case of this and a packet of Capstan Full Strength Navy Cut in my cargo[8]. If I'd just spent 12 hours hauling herring off the Dogger Bank, this is what I'd turn to for the required robust, full-flavoured, absolutely massive assault on the senses.

I'd imagine that this is what Long John Silver, Stevenson's one-legged gentleman of fortune, would drink, especially if he'd just dug up a chest of blood-soaked gold doubloons. So, let's be clear: we're not looking at subtlety here, but I confess that I loved this from the first drop (well, possibly the second; the first rather took my breath away because I hadn't spotted the 57% ABV strength and drank with more enthusiasm than discretion). It's packed with notes of muscovado sugar, toffee and cloves and it's reassuringly, authentically dark. For around £25 you simply can't go wrong.

Wood's is now owned by William Grant & Sons (we met them at the entry for Sailor Jerry) and distilled for them in Guyana to the original navy recipe in a 250-year-old wooden pot still – and there aren't many of those left, I can tell you.

But perhaps those Hoxton hipsters will love it. I can personally guarantee this will put hairs on their chins.

---

8   With apologies to John Masefield.

100

ZACAPA 23

Brand owner: Industrias Licoreras de Guatemala
Website: www.zacaparum.com
Origin: Guatemala

ZACAPA, IN CASE YOU WERE WONDERING, IS A TOWN IN EASTERN
Guatemala, and the straw band round the base of the bottle is a
petate – traditionally, a hand-woven palm mat used in bedding and
hat production. That settled we can move on.

The bold 23 on the bottle once referred, rather misleadingly, to the
age of the rum. If you're used to Scotch whisky and saw the large
numeral, you'd take it to indicate the age, but as we have learned (if
you were paying attention), rum doesn't work quite like that.

But since global giant Diageo took over distribution of Zacapa, the
'23 Años' wording has been quietly dropped and replaced by the
words 'Sistema Solera'. Not only is that more honest, it begins to tell
us something interesting about this jolly fine product.

There's quite a complex distillation and maturation regime behind
it: first the rum is distilled at the sugar mill from concentrated
first-pressing sugar cane juice – that's the 'virgin sugar cane honey'
on the label – then moved to a blending facility in the Guatemalan
highlands, at an altitude of around 7,500 feet, where the climate is
more stable, the temperature lower and the rum will mature more
slowly. This they style the 'House Above the Clouds' – you will have
observed their penchant for romantic copy.

It then gets even more complex, because four different types of casks
are used in a solera-type system, then there is a giant marrying cask
where rums aged between six and 23 years are blended together for a
year, after which the rum is sweetened and then bottled.

But what you want to know before splashing a cool £50 or so on a
bottle, is – is it worth it?

Well, a lot of knowledgeable people think so. Zacapa 23 has
won a hatful of awards and regularly picks up plaudits from the
cognoscenti. You can mix it, of course, but for my money this is one
to sip and savour.

The company themselves suggest that it is 'best enjoyed on a single
large lump of pure, clear ice in a luxury rocks glass with a heavy base'.
If that strikes you as overly specific, I expect any old glass would do.
I won't tell.

101

ZACAPA EDICIÓN NEGRA

Brand owner: Industrias Licoreras de Guatemala
Website: www.zacaparum.com
Origin: Guatemala

APPARENTLY, SOMEONE IS PLANNING A RUM DISTILLERY ON ISLAY – you know, the Hebridean island where the peaty whiskies come from. At the time of writing I don't have any more details, but you might now find something on the web.

It came to mind because this unusual rum struck me as the kind of thing that the 'smokeheads' might like if they wanted something a little subtler than the roaring, peat-soaked, phenolic monsters from Scotland's West Coast. Because this is a rum with a smoky finish.

It was first sold in tax-free markets (that's airports and ferries for most of the hoi polloi, unless you have access to the fabulous riches of the legendary diplomatic stores that our representatives who lie abroad[9] for their country are said to frequent) but it is now more widely available.

If you've read the previous page you'll realise that, with its added dose of sugar, Zacapa is on the sweet side, but this is rather different and the sugar hit has been cut markedly. Many drinkers will welcome this.

The trick here has been to take the regular Zacapa, already delicious, and age it in double-charred American oak casks. The result is greater intensity, a pleasing, slightly bitter note dancing around the dark brown sugar, and great dollops of coffee, dark chocolate, woodsmoke and fiery spices. It's said that Master Blender Lorena Vasquez, a veteran of 25 years in the industry, was 'inspired by the natural elements of Guatemala and the dark fire of its volcanoes' – though I can't help noticing that brand partners Diageo have done something similar with one or two of their single malt whiskies.

This is a really great addition to any rum portfolio, which, apart from the fairly stiff retail price, I feel able to recommend with enthusiasm. It was launched at €70 in duty free shops and that's certainly a considered purchase. However, if you like slightly smoky and quite intense flavours, then grab a bottle. You won't get burnt (apart from Sir Henry Wooton's footnote that's the last dreadful pun – and it was intended; sorry).

The other two Zacapas, XO and Royal, are somewhat more expensive and largely restricted to tax free outlets, but well worth the effort it takes to find them.

---

9   "An ambassador is an honest gentleman sent to lie abroad for the good of his country." Sir Henry Wooton, 1604. Rather a clever pun I always think.

Acknowledgements

Along with the dream team of Judy Moir (agent) and Neville Moir (publisher), I dreamt up this book over a glass of hot malted milk (and if you believe that…). So it's their fault. Judy eventually put the deal together with her customary imperturbable charm, tact and attention to detail.

Very special thanks to Ben Ellefsen, Anna Grant and their colleagues at the Master of Malt website, who have kindly helped out by providing many of the illustrations (all copyrights are acknowledged). The vintage labels and other illustrations on pages 6, 8, 11, 13, 14, 17, 18-19 and 223 appear courtesy of The Scotch Whisky Archive. All Rights Reserved.

Teresa Monachino of Studio Monachino turned the whole thing into this good looking book

Quite a few companies generously provided samples and will, I hope, be happy to see their brands appearing here. However – and here's a top tip – I also bought (*bought*, please note) a considerable number of tasting samples from the Master of Malt website, where 3 cl mini bottles of many fine spirits are available at reasonable cost (other tasting services are available). When I wasn't quite sure about a particular entry this enabled me to make a quick evaluation and avoid the embarrassment of soliciting a sample only to reject it for inclusion (one so hates upsetting PR folk). It also greatly hastened the process of writing this book. I hope that you like it.